"OF CABBAGES AND KINGS"

7. Meconopsis Baileyii, or more correctly, Meconopsis "betonicifolia"

# "OF CABBAGES AND KINGS"

*by*

T. C. MANSFIELD

WITH ILLUSTRATIONS FROM
NATURAL COLOUR PHOTOGRAPHS

*by*

JOHN HINDE

Collins

14 ST. JAMES'S PLACE LONDON

1945

To
KEITH
*with much hope*

*"The time has come," the Walrus said,*
*"To talk of many things,*
*Of shoes, of ships, of sealing wax,*
*Of Cabbages and Kings."*

LEWIS CARROLL.

COPYRIGHT
PRINTED IN GREAT BRITAIN
COLLINS CLEAR-TYPE PRESS : LONDON AND GLASGOW
1945

# Contents

# Plates

# Preface

THE presentation of a book like this must be, in wartime, a matter of some speculation. Asked how such a book should be illustrated, the answer was given spontaneously, "In colour," for I am convinced that the real interest of the gardener lies in visual rather than gastronomic satisfaction.

In our previous books Hinde and I have tried to satisfy no particular aesthetic sense, since these books were mainly encyclopaedic. Here, however, we have catered from the point of view of art rather than artifice.

In books previously illustrated by John Hinde he has paid considerable attention to accuracy of colour, and this accuracy has been maintained; but in the present book he has used the medium of colour photography more as a craft to give expression to art.

It may be argued that this is more fittingly the work of the painter, who is bound less by conventions than is the photographer. But I feel sure that if the reader will spend a few moments in contemplation of the picture of the seed heads of *Clematis macropetala* (illustrated in Plate X.) he will agree that artistry is not the sole prerogative of the man with the palette.

The scope of the present volume is large; thus it cannot hope to illustrate in any great measure many of the multifarious plants it mentions. It is, however, an honest attempt to present in popular fashion a wide survey of a subject dear to our hearts. Let us not in an era of expediency lose sight of real values. Beauty of colour, line, of mind and of soul must be retained.

For my part I have enjoyed the tedium of the production of this little book. It arose in part from a series of questions put to me by Mr. W. A. R. Collins and answers. I hope the questions you would all like to ask.

A revision will doubtless be called for at a more opportune stage and I shall welcome your letters at the appended address, and will endeavour at some future time to answer your enquiries.

I should like to pay tribute to the unfailing patience of my colleague, John Hinde, who has generally encouraged its production.

One of the most helpful features of previous works has been the correspondence I have received from service men throughout the world: the gardeners of the past and future. I can only say that their appreciation of my efforts pales into insignificance when I regard theirs, and as an ex-soldier and a gardener I am quite sure they demonstrate that nothing can evolve in the course of the struggle for life unless it shows an overall, marked improvement upon that which preceded it.

My father, to whom I owe a debt of gratitude for my inheritance of a love for gardening, frequently used as an admonition: "I never did that when I was a boy," meant, I am afraid, in the sense that my own actions were retrogressive rather than progressive.

I am certain I can only echo his words, but in a rather more appreciative manner; for only too sincerely I feel that the present generation has so far outstripped its parents that even if I tried I "could not have done that when I was a boy!"

I will add, however, that if a book like this one can help to while away an hour or two, or can help to stimulate a love for the beautiful, or to bring back to the war-worn mind a consciousness of things waiting beyond the present, then both Hinde and I shall have accomplished in bountiful measure what we set out to do with some diffidence and doubt.

GLASTONBURY,
    SOMERSET, APRIL, 1944.

# Chapter One

## OF GARDENERS AND GARDENS

"And who are *these*?" said the Queen, pointing to the three gardeners who were lying round the rose tree; for you see, as they were lying on their faces, and the patterns on their backs were the same as the rest of the pack, she could not tell whether they were gardeners, or soldiers, or courtiers or three of her own children."

LEWIS CARROLL.

LIFE is too short to make any one of us a perfect gardener. Equally fortunately, the human race is not sufficiently old for gardeners to be born perfect. Thus in the great garden of the universe, amid sunshine and shadow, in calm and storm, beset with giants and dwarfs, fighting pestilence and profusion, famine and fertility, the gardener must go his slow way to produce a fitting home for all the lovely things of earth, adding thereby to his own stature, while his charges spread before him the riches of the universe in unbounded generosity.

Was it Alexander who sighed for other worlds to conquer? Let the gardener be thankful for his present imperfections, for the science of gardening aims as much at improving the gardener as the garden. Shall he sit back and sigh for better things; shall he gather together his tools, his books and his mother wit, and evict the weeds, encourage the weak, prune (perhaps but lightly) the strong, be firm with pests, train giants and dwarfs to live in harmony, with that slow but certain progress which makes it certain that neither he nor his garden will ever be perfect, since the gardener lives to tend, to train, to experiment, to prune and to improve, and with perfection with which to start, how could this be?

Let us learn from our mistakes as we proceed and mould our garden so that its dwellers are flourishing and content and growing in beauty from year to year, and from century to century.

These gardeners are good men, and good women. There are no bad gardeners, but there are no perfect gardeners, for which fact I re-echo a previously expressed sentiment "Thank goodness." The leisurely science is one in which one reaches a rich regard for one's own ignorance just when life has begun its ebb, and one crowds into each minute the experience of two, to mend one's leisure and ignorance simultaneously.

But these good gardeners, who are they?

The first who comes to mind was a Cockney coster with a bright green barrow. His barrow was a real joy, and he was a king! I never knew his name, but his smile identified him and his cheery chatter rendered him unforgettable, so much that I never associate the particular corner of the East End where his barrow usually rested with any other thing. But why, you ask, do I think he was a good gardener? I can only give you one answer to that. He loved plants. Never even during the hottest spring days would you find his plants wilting, never would you see him handle them roughly; always would he handle them firmly, but wrap them with care, and for months afterwards he would inquire about their well-being from his many customers. He always knew the names of his plants and though he could not spell, he certainly could write, for the memory still sticks in my mind of the large label which adorned and graced a box of seedling wallflowers, the botanical name of which as you are aware is *Cheiranthus*, and which bore the cryptic but lovely name CHERRY ANTHERS. From him we may learn much.

The second good gardener was a chimney sweep who, curiously enough, also lived in the East End of London—and what gardeners these Londoners are! I shall not forget him, poor fellow, long since he has been gardening in a more promising garden. Imagine a patch of garden approximately sixteen feet wide by twelve feet long, on the south side of the street because (to quote him) "They wouldn't get no sun" on the other side of the road, peopled by the most amazing plants which ever grew. Three hundred yards away was situated a factory which produced sulphuric acid in vast quantities, with its consequent fumes, and within thirty yards ran the railway with its locomotives belching soot and fumes, which coated all growing things with a layer of soot, which would leave a thick black stain on all which touched it. My chimney sweep friend knew, however, that however good sulphates might be as fertilisers, sulphuric acid as an aid to a plant's complexion was literally a defacer, and that, however good soot might be as a means of earning an honest living and discouraging slugs and pests, it was undesirable when applied thickly to foliage. He therefore sponged his plants clean as often as he could, and sprayed them when time allowed to keep them clean and able to breathe. He too loved plants.

My next good gardener was a Scotswoman. She too lived in the East End, and here I apologise if I give the impression that all good gardeners are dwellers in East London. I remember her name quite well—it was MacRoberts; she had reached her seventieth year, but was as able and nimble in her garden as if she were the comely seventeen she must have been in youth. Every year her garden lived again under the careful tutelage of her hands. She grew nothing but annuals which she raised from seed. Each year she grew something new, something she had never grown before, and I can still remember the thrilling tones she used when telling of another new discovery raised from a penny packet! I should put the annual cost of her garden at something less than five shillings a year, and its profit to the neighbourhood at something greater than the National Debt. She not only made her seeds grow, she encouraged the growth of other gardeners, and gradually what was really a dismal row of back gardens brightened by only one fair garden became first two, then three, and finally forty-nine out of the fifty-two back-yards (the other three were empty houses) became coloured with patches of sunshine, pools of sky, gouts of flame, and sweeps of grass. The Scots are not only good gardeners, they are grand pioneers! My good gardeners were all very humble people. Did not Mahomet say, "He that hath two cakes of bread, let him sell one of them for some flowers of the *Narcissus*; for bread is food for the body, but Narcissus is food for the soul"?

I like to think that the gardener cares more for the process of feeding the soul than for the important function of feeding the body, and can find no sight which transcends in beauty the picture of a tiny child cupping in its palms a handful of the sunshine given to the world by the Celandine, for it is from this we can gather hope in the knowledge that beauty in any guise will continue to appeal to even the least sophisticated of us all.

Probably quite erroneously I prefer to believe that Scott's lines—

> "Breathes there a man with soul so dead
> Who never to himself hath said
> This is my own, my native land."

refer not to an inborn patriotism but a love for that piece of ground which every man has tilled, and cultivated, and loved. This is a spirit common to all humanity, irrespective of race, and can provide a bond stronger than any other tie. The expressions of gardening are universal; nothing else encourages men to be so generous, so eager to share with others in nature's bounty, to accept her rebuffs, and to triumph over all difficulties, and so to all men of goodwill we should add to "Let us pray"—"and let us dig."

I have called gardening "the leisurely science" firstly because a large proportion of the time spent in the garden should be spent in contemplation. The true gardener is not the slave who labours from dawn to dusk upon his lawns, his cabbages, his roses, or his rock garden. He takes stock from time to time of his performance, he considers how this feature or that may be improved, he ponders his successes and his failures, and correlates from year to year his practice with his attainments. Thus he learns but slowly, but he learns mainly from experiment and the inevitable procession of cause and effect.

I have written elsewhere that "the good gardener has every reason to be as proud of the performance of his hands as the great pianist." This might well be amplified to embrace also the translation into reality of his imagination, and the substantiation of his dreams, for in addition to performance the gardener must be gifted with vision, in fact with prevision. The ability to foresee the future is given to few, but the gardener who plans gradually acquires the art of foreseeing the ultimate visual effect of a project which in its embryonic stages conveys only to the brain its final appearance.

Let us return, however, to gardeners. A story is told of George Russell, the able producer of the now well-known Russell Lupins, watching the departure for the first time of four of his specimen plants for a Horticultural Show on a horse-drawn coal cart, with tears in his eyes. Whether this story is authentic or not, I am not prepared to say, but it certainly helps to demonstrate the essential characteristic of all gardeners; but lest you should be led away into believing that love of plants means the tolerance of something less better than the best, you must also consider Russell's ruthlessness in destroying many thousands of second rate seedlings so that the surviving strain might become still better.

Another story illustrates a further characteristic of the good gardener. During the last Chelsea Flower Show in 1939, a dear old lady wandered around the marquees, absorbing all the wonders, gazing at Antirrhinums which were in some cases eight feet in height, peering at rare orchids which had all the exotic appearance of the ultra-sophisticated. As she passed I heard her remark to a friend, "Wonderful, wonderful, but you should see my Aspidistra!"

This remark I may add was not intended to be facetious. Pride of possession is essentially a part of the gardener's ensemble, and while it cannot be said that the angler has the monopoly of tall stories, for who has not read each year in the newspapers the comparative growth of Brown's or Smith's hollyhocks, it is no part of the gardener's make-up to indulge in exaggeration. Quite often the production of a plant microscopically small can give a greater measure of satisfaction than the production of a coarse giant.

I cannot better illustrate a still further attribute of the good gardener than by quoting from a letter I have recently received from a very gallant and brave woman. I should explain that she was a very keen Alpine gardener and devoted much of her leisure to the cultivation of tiny plants, with great success and much pleasure. During the past two years she has begun to lose her sight to such an extent that she can no longer see small objects. She writes in her letter as an afterthought, "I must

begin to grow giant sunflowers." Can we not also learn much
from this, not only of the art of gardening but also of the art
of living?

My son, at the beginning of the slope of life—he is just two
years of age—spends the greater part of his awareness in the
garden. He distinguishes between plants and weeds and has
definite preferences for some flowers from others, generally call-
ing them by names invented by himself, but definitely keeping
the same name for identical flowers. He, too, realises the need
for some measure of orderliness, and I am quite sure will in
course of time prove himself a real gardener.

What then are the mental needs of the gardener? He must
first of all be a lover of plants; he must be a pioneer; he must
be a lover of beauty; he must upon occasion be ruthless; he
must be thoughtful and not impetuous; he must be patient;
he must have imagination; he must be manually facile; he
must have pride of possession; he must be observant; he must
be orderly. Must he then be a superman? No, for surely this
mental equipment is just that possessed by the average man or
woman, and he who suffers from a slight deficiency in one
respect will have added sufficiency in another respect. Gardening is essentially the ideal leisure occupation for every human
capable of coherent thought.

So far I have not mentioned physique, or physical strength.
Is this gardening a hobby for the strong, for who but the strong
shall dig? Who needs to dig a garden? Your garden may be a
yard square or a mile square to match your capacity for hard
work. I know a garden, which for years I have called the pocket-
handkerchief garden, tended solely by its owner who is over
eighty years of age. This garden is but eighteen yards square,
and contains every feature of the grander and greater gardens,
including rose-beds, pools, rock gardens, shrubberies, and herbaceous borders and lawns. The proportions of the construction
are perfect, and the planting is in keeping. The work of main-
tenance is not great but requires considerable patience and
regular attention.

I know two folk whose only gardening is done in window
boxes, with great success; others who grow what they can in
bowls, and others who employ many gardeners to tend their

1. "Keith," one of the youngest of gardeners

many acres. Can any of these be said to dig? Nevertheless they are gardeners. I am far from convinced that the gardener need dig at all, but we will talk about that at a later stage. Suffice it to say for the present that one of the greatest attractions of the science and art of gardening is that one can estimate one's own capacity, and prove oneself conservative by constantly exceeding one's own estimate.

As with the gardener, so with the garden. No garden can be intrinsically bad. It may be ill planned, and ill conceived, it may lack colour, character and charm, but it will be an expression of opinion: the opinion of its constructor, and it will contain somewhere, in perhaps the least expected spot, a redeeming feature which to the discerning eye will obliterate all its obvious deficiencies.

I dislike, and this is merely an expression of personal opinion, all formal beds which contain shall we say red geraniums, white marguerites, blue lobelias, and yellow calceolarias. Regimented plants to my mind belong to the nursery beds. I had occasion some years ago to visit a garden in which closely clipped lawns were neatly studded with a host of geometrical beds, each making a violent assault upon the retina. The gardener responsible had literally worked miracles, for originally only two inches below the surface of the soil was a bed of solid limestone, which here and there had cropped out upon the surface.

Every bed had meant days of sweat and toil, but the work had been done. Soil had been imported, rock had been removed, and orderliness prevailed—but for one spot. Here nature had provided a large outcrop of rock which dynamite alone could have removed. Faced with an insuperable difficulty, the gardener had given it up, and into the cracks and crannies in the rocks he had inserted seeds and seedlings of all the trailing and creeping plants he could remember, and had created a garden of beauty which he knew at once to be good, for he looked at it with pride and said: "Do you know, I feel glad now that I could not level it like the rest."

The most attractive gardens do not just grow or evolve, they are the result of careful and orderly planning. This planning may sometimes be quite unconscious, or rather sub-conscious, and its involuntary unfoldment surprises even its originator.

The fact still remains that they are an expression of ideas which may never have taken anything but an abstract shape in the mind.

The worst gardens like the worst houses are those which have periodic additions. Though many can be very good, the majority show signs of their patchwork origin, and rarely become a coherent whole. It is not implied that all work upon a garden should be done simultaneously, but merely that it should be fully planned before any extensive work is undertaken.

## Chapter Two

### OF CATALOGUES AND NAMES

"Speak English," said the Eaglet. "I don't know the meaning of half of these long words, and what's more, I don't believe you do either."

LEWIS CARROLL.

ONE of the greatest causes of alarm to the tyro in the art of gardening, more real than all the pests and diseases which lurk in hiding, seeking whom they may devour, are the names found in gardening catalogues and books, which at first sight appear to be another method of enshrouding a universal profession with a cloak of mystery. How can one fail to be aghast at such names as Myriophyllum proserpinacoides? This prompts in the reader's mind the thought that the gardening public would be increased if a larger measure of simplicity could be obtained. At first sight this view would seem to be well founded, but there are a number of reasons why it is impracticable.

Names are given to plants so that when they are either spoken or written, there shall be no misunderstanding as to which particular plant it refers to. It is, therefore, essential that every plant shall bear one name only which must be of universal acceptance. For this reason the International Horticultural Conferences held in London in 1930, Paris in 1932, Rome in 1935, and Berlin in 1938, have generally agreed upon the basic principles to be used in the naming of plants. These set out that for plants of garden origin the principles were that a plant could have but one valid name which should be the earliest that conformed to the accepted rules of nomenclature. Names, species, and botanical varieties are framed according to the rules of the nomenclature set up by the Botanical Congress of Vienna in 1905, and revised at the Congress of Brussels in 1910, Cambridge in 1930 and Amsterdam in 1935.

Set out briefly, the name of a species should consist of two words in Latin form. The first is the name of the genus to which the plant belongs and is written with a capital initial letter; the second, which is the earliest specific name given by Linnaeus in 1753 or by other botanists after that date, is written with a small initial letter unless the specific name is derived from the name of a person, or is that of another genus. This generally is the code of rules accepted in the naming of plants, and there are many good reasons why this procedure is more important than would appear at first sight.

To begin with, it is essential that the names of garden plants shall be universal and for this reason it is necessary to adopt a language which can be of universal acceptance. For this reason the names are based upon either Latin or Greek. This enables the names to be condensed into a reasonable length, though they normally convey a very definite meaning. Often the criticism is applied that it would be much simpler to use the common English names of the plants rather than the Latin generic names. But even if it were decided to use the common names applied to plants by the English-speaking races, we should find that certain of them used in this country were quite different from those used for the same plant in America, and to make confusion worse confounded we should find that the common English names applied to more than one plant.

For the purposes of classification plants have been divided into groups, the smallest group of which is given to the species. This is a group of plants which breeds true to a certain number of characteristics but which may have certain variations such as a difference of colour, or of height, present among its various component plants. Where it is considered necessary, these individual variations which breed true are given varietal names.

The species are again grouped into genera, among which the components have a wider resemblance one to the other than they bear to the members of another genus. The genera are distinguished by the differences in the composition of the reproductive organ of the plant.

Genera which have limited resemblances one to another are grouped into still larger groups which are termed families.

The generic name may have a particular reference to some specific characteristic of the genus. For instance the name *Erigeron* arises from the characteristic fluffy seed-head of the plant, which resembles the greying head of an old man, from the Greek from which the name is derived. The family *Compositae*, or Daisy family, to which the genus *Erigeron* belongs, is the largest of all the families, comprising upwards of eight hundred genera, the resemblance of one to the other being contained in the assemblage of the individual flowers joined round the pistil, the corolla with its petals joined at the base, sometimes produced into a long limb on one side, but usually present in two forms in the one head. In addition the stamens number from four to five and the seed vessel is below the corolla and is made up of a small cell.

Such widely diverse genera as Centaurea, Carlina, Chrysanthemum, Dahlia, Gaillardia, Helichrysum, Lactuca, Petasites, Santolina, and Zinnia are found among the members of the family, but even to the uninitiated the family resemblance is obvious.

From this it will be seen that specific generic and family names of the plant are no mere tags, but that each plays its part in assigning the plant to the group of plants which it most closely resembles, and with which it has some community of descent.

I am frequently told that many plant names are quite as frightening and sound rather more like the names of diseases than of flowers. I cannot agree that this is so, but then I have lived for so many years with these plant names that they have become like a family to me.

An attempt was made some time ago to anglicise certain of the generic names and as an example the name Saxifrage became the name Rockfoil. Saxifrage has a very definite meaning; Rockfoil has none. In any case it would seem unwise to coin such words when the word Saxifrage has become part and parcel of everyday gardener's language. If an attempt was made to continue this process throughout the whole of the genera, we should find ourselves with some difficult hurdles to surmount. To anglicise Nemophila linifolia, we should have to translate it literally as "the inhabitant of the wood with narrow leaves", or to follow a very bad example already set us, "the narrow-leaved wood-foil." The absurdity of this treatment speaks for itself. Nor will the use of the common English name prove any more useful or beautiful. The genus we know as Erigeron has the English equivalent of Fleabane, but we can find a number of other plants which also carry this common name since it was important in earlier times to know that an extract from such plants could be used as an encouragement to personal cleanliness. To-day this no longer applies. Erigeron is itself descriptive; it indicates that the seed-head of the plant is tasselled and hoary like the head of an old man, and as such helps us to identify the genus. Moreover even from the point of view of musical speech Erigeron undoubtedly sounds better and trips more lightly from the tongue than its English equivalent. Even when one comes to such a fascinating common name as the Dog's Tooth Violet one has an equally fascinating alternative in the pleasant sounding scientific name of Erythronium. And who would prefer the commoner or simpler name of Swamp Lily to the charming Zephyranthes, which has its literal translation "The Flower of the South-West Wind?"

So far we have seen that these scientific names have a meaning, and it is essential that this should be so. I hold no brief for naming plants to confer honour upon the discoverer or originator of a plant, and it is far better that a plant should bear its name because it is descriptive than that a rose should suffer by being called Frau Karl Druschki instead of "Snow Queen", which its raiser originally intended to call it. What can be said for Alonsoa Warscewiczii, which is purely commemorative and cannot be said to be classical in intention?

The pronunciation of such names adds difficulties which the ordinary gardener may find it hard to overcome, especially when one realises that there are two accepted ways to pronounce the Greek ones. This, of course, is a magnificent excuse for failing to pronounce any one correctly! Quite obviously the person of common sense, synonym for good gardener, would not dream of talking of 'HyaKinthus' instead of 'HyaCinthus', or 'NarKissus' instead of 'NarCissus', or 'GAum' instead of 'GEum', since these words have become part and parcel of the English language. The simplest way to overcome the difficulty with one's friends is to have the name written upon a label and when asked to air one's knowledge of the name of the plant to produce the written label and hand it over with a triumphant "There you are!" but often this method fails, since the question almost invariably comes back: "How do you say it?" and thus returns to plague the inventor.

How are these names decided? Their adoption or rejection is the work of the International Committee which has as its guiding principle that of priority. If, for instance, a plant was named in the year 1752 by John Smith, for example Azalea Smithii, and five years later by John Brown, Azalea Brownii, the Committee would undoubtedly decide that the real name should be Azalea Smithii. It is exceedingly probable that, although new plants are constantly being discovered in many parts of the world, some have been previously collected and named by an earlier discoverer. If the second name were allowed to stand in any one instance, it would form a fine precedent for continuing to change the name of any plant at the slightest provocation, and we should find the honest but hardly tried nurseryman, after having failed to sell his plant as Azalea Brownii, change it in the following year to Azalea Robinsonii in the hope that the discerning public would find it more attractive in its new garb. And so when you find the names in your catalogue and in your gardening books a little disconcerting, give a thought to the fact that they take the shape they do as much for your protection and enlightenment as they do for identification, and thus make it easy for you to obtain the plant which appeals to you artistically equally well from any one of many hundreds of growers.

And now for catalogues. It is strange that 90 per cent of the plants and seeds which are sold each year are bought as the result of postal communication between members of the public and the grower. For this reason it is necessary that the grower shall produce a catalogue describing the wares which he has to sell. A catalogue may vary from a single sheet of paper to a book running into many hundreds of pages. Often it reflects the personal opinion of the grower; sometimes it reflects the personal opinion of the Company or Agency which compiled it; sometimes it contains descriptions which are plucked from encyclopaedias and other books of the same type; sometimes it contains barefaced attempts to dispose of something to an unsuspecting public which the public have previously shown themselves unwilling to acquire. On the whole, however, none of these things is the case. As a rule the normal catalogue is a truthful and exact account of the appearance and general characteristics of the plant, and may be trusted not unduly to 'gild the lily.' No catalogue offers so much to its possessor as the normal gardening catalogue. It is full of hints, and of advice and generally contains between its two covers a wealth of wisdom given gratuitously.

Catalogues, however, must be used intelligently. More often than not the grower will point out the idiosyncrasies of various plants and trees and shrubs. He will go to the trouble of telling his prospective customers that such and such a plant requires to be grown in a certain kind of soil. He does this because he knows that it is bad business from his point of view to sell goods to people who will fail with them mainly because the conditions which the buyers can offer will be unable to satisfy the natural requirements of the plants. The grower knows that his public is highly intelligent and does not need to be told that it must also provide for the plant means by which it is to feed and grow. It is not enough to express a wish to grow a certain plant, or in other words to buy it, in order to make it grow successfully. The elementary precaution which the buyer can take is to make sure that the conditions he can offer his welcome guest will make it happy and contented and imbue it with a desire to stay with him for all time.

Many catalogues, especially those issued in happier days, contain illustrations both in black and white and in colour of the wares they advertise. These illustrations were, as a rule, the most accurate which could at those times be produced. Unfortunately, mechanical reproduction of pictures in colour could not be said to be remarkably accurate, and it would be unwise always to assume that the actual colours illustrated would be those of the plant when it was successfully grown. This is particularly true of such things as roses, which are extraordinarily difficult to portray upon paper since one cannot counterfeit in colour the texture of the living petal, and in order to compensate for a lack of natural glow, brightness in colour was added to make the illustration stand out and look attractive, as it is an elementary precaution for the grower incorporating colour pictures in his catalogue to see that such a procedure renders his goods more enticing.

Catalogues, to be really useful, should not state opinions on the subject of colour but should try, as far as possible, to give an accurate indication of the colour of a flower, since colour sense is a matter entirely of personal taste which can sometimes overrun even good sense. To illustrate this I quote the story of a woman who wished to engage a gardener. After a great deal of correspondence with one of the candidates, which had got down to the stage of discussing terms, she added in her last letter as a postscript: "I won't have you if you have brown eyes." So a brown-eyed gardener looked for a job elsewhere, and the prospect of a grey or blue-eyed gardener added a little pleasure to the rather unhappy sphere occupied by this poor woman. This is an extreme case of personal taste in colour.

There are a number of people who profess a profound horror for flowers which are magenta in colour. There is no question that this horror does exist in a very real sense, and I have often tried to find the main offending factor giving rise to this peculiar aversion. Could it be that such colours could hurt the optic nerves, or is it a question of mere personal dislike? Personal contact with a large number of individuals of this kind has led me to suppose that there is a large range of colour on either side of the magenta colour band which does annoy a good many people; but in most individual cases the range is not large, and in the case of different individuals is not always found in the same place in the spectrum band. I have actually come across people who objected to Primula rosea because it was magenta, and others who raised their hands in horror at Primula Poissonii for the same reason; while others found Calandrinia umbellata a perfectly fascinating colour, decrying at the same time, Primula Beesiana. I have come to the conclusion, therefore, that it is the peculiar combination of red and blue in certain proportions to which the largest number of people object, and that the proportion of the offending blue varies with different individuals.

Nor can one divorce the colour of the plant from the colour of the surroundings. Primula Beesiana, illustrated in Plate II, shows how a magenta colour can be quite attractive with a wild green background, and I would suggest that the repulsiveness of certain colours arises more by reason of their associations than from their actual colours, and should urge those who find certain colours to their distaste to experiment with them in other surroundings.

# Chapter Three

## OF AGE

"Indeed, she had quite a long argument with the Lory, who at last turned sulky, and would only say, "I am older than you and must know better"; and this Alice would not allow without knowing how old it was, and as the Lory positively refused to tell its age, there was no more to be said."

LEWIS CARROLL.

IN addition to the division of plants into families, genera, and species, the gardener has empirically divided plants into three classes, which he has for want of a better name called annuals, biennials, and perennials. Within all these classes considerable variations in the length of life can be found.

The general definition given to an annual is that it is a plant which will last for one year only; but this is not necessarily true of all the plants which the gardener dubs "annual". Probably a better definition is that it is a plant which can bloom in the first year of its life, after which it dies.

Annuals we divide into three sections, which again for want of better names, we shall call "Hardy Annuals", "Half-hardy Annuals", and "Tender Annuals." Of the first class we may quote the Marigold (*Tagetes erecta*), Cornflower (*Centaurea cyanus*), the Larkspur (*Delphinium Ajacis*), and the Sweet Pea (*Lathyrus odoratus*).

Of the second class we may quote the China Aster (*Callistephus chinensis*), *Nemesia strumosa*, and *Petunia hybrida*.

Of the third class it is sufficient to quote *Mesembryanthemum tricolor*.

It must be obvious to the reader that the life of any of these types of plants can vary considerably, for it is possible, and for that matter desirable, that the hardy (or winter) annual should be sown in the autumn of the year preceding that in which it

is required to flower. Under these conditions the plant matures
earlier and flowers more continuously and prolifically than if it
is sown in the following spring.

The half-hardy annuals are sown in the spring and continue
to flower only as long as climatic conditions and the approach
of senility will allow.

The Tender annuals are generally raised under frame or
greenhouse conditions, or sown when weather conditions are
suitable for their continued growth. Thus the total life span of
the hardy annuals may be as long as fourteen months, the life-
span of the half-hardy annuals may be only slightly in excess of
six months, and that of the tender annuals no greater than four
months.

Many plants which possess perennial qualities under more
favourable weather conditions are grown as half-hardy or tender
annuals; such a one is Diascia Barbarae, but the true annual
is the plant which can complete its whole life-cycle in one
season.

Certain hardy annuals may be persuaded to flourish for
many years provided they are not allowed to flower, and
will under these conditions grow into large and almost
shrublike plants which may last for as long as six or seven
years. This can be easily demonstrated with such a plant as
Mignonette.

Monocarpic plants which are really perennial in that they
persist for longer than two years, are those which take longer
than a single season to complete their life-cycle, but die after
flowering. The text-book example of this kind of plant is
*Corypha umbraculifera*, a fan palm which is a native of the Malabar
coast and Ceylon. It can attain an age of eighty years before it
flowers, fruits, and dies.

The genus Meconopsis contains among its specific varieties a
number of monocarpic species varying very considerably in
their life-span. Meconopsis regia for instance often attains the
age of five years before it flowers—only to die. Meconopsis
betonicaefolia can also be either perennial or monocarpic, according to the circumstances under which it is grown. If allowed
to flower at too early an age it is definitely monocarpic. If prevented from flowering during its second year of life by being

"stopped," it produces offsets and continues to persist as a perennial.

It would appear that the production of the flowers and fruits of certain varieties subjects the structure of the plant to a strain which may be fatal, whatever the actual mechanics of the fruition may be. This is why the gardener "dead-ends" his plants after flowering, so that the structure may not be greatly weakened by the production of unwanted seed. If such a procedure encourages a further recrudescence of flowering, the heart of the gardener is gladdened, as it should be, but such flowering probably induces a similar strain which does not help to prolong the life or strengthen the growth of the plant.

Popular opinion imputes to the definition perennial the ability of a plant to "live for ever." This is incorrect. The secret of immortality is as much concealed from the plant as it is from the human being and even perennial plants have a definite life-span, although it varies considerably.

Trees like Sequoia sempervirens—the Redwood—are reputed to live for 2000 to 4000 years, but the Scots Pine rarely exceeds 150 years. Thus we must not expect all our perennial plants to persist indefinitely. Even within a genus the life-span of the member can be very variable. In the genus *Dianthus*, for instance, we have found that the members of the barbatus group, comprising such varieties as Napoleon III and Spark, are very short-lived, rarely exceeding four years.

Fortunately by means of vegetative reproduction new plants, containing less of the old and tired structures, can be obtained, and by such means a strong and healthy stock kept from year to year while the older plants pass down the path to oblivion.

In the case of trees, shrubs and plants in which the wood persists from year to year it cannot be said that the whole of the structure is alive. As the plant ages progressively, the innermost structures of the wood are dying, and are being replaced by new, living outer tissues.

With trees, in particular, decay of the inner wood may begin, and eventually little but the outer living tissues may remain, though the tree continues to live, bearing leaves and flowers and fruit in an apparently normal fashion. By detaching the younger parts of plants which are of considerable age and are reaching the limit of their normal life-span, and encouraging them to produce roots of their own, as the gardener does when he takes cuttings, a new entity of more youthful structure is obtained and the life-span of the species increased. This kind of propagation is comparable to the passage of living structure to the offspring by the parent.

In a similar way, division of the hard, woody roots of herbaceous plants encourages the production of new and virile roots, unencumbered with old dead tissues which are subject to decay, and consequently transmit disease to the younger structures.

In their turn the families, genera, and species exhibit certain transformations at different seasons, facts which have led the gardener to describe the species as evergreen, deciduous, and herbaceous.

Within the family, the genera may show marked differences, one genus proving wholly evergreen, another consisting entirely of deciduous and herbaceous plants. Within the genus also there may be a wide range of differences. For instance the genus Veronica numbers among its species herbaceous, deciduous and evergreen plants, and at least one species, Veronica Hulkeana, which can be either herbaceous or evergreen, according to the circumstances under which it is grown. In certain cases, notably the common Beech, the tree cannot be said to be evergreen since the leaves wither but persist, and cannot therefore be said to be deciduous, except when fully grown.

Deciduous and herbaceous plants shed their leaves as a protection from undue evaporation. During winter, generally a season of high winds, and possibly of frozen water-supplies in the ground, evaporation would, because of the mechanical disturbance, take place at a greater rate than could be readily replenished, with disastrous results to the plant, though under normal conditions the stomata through which transpiration takes place have a tendency to close before actual wilting occurs.

Evergreen plants, trees and shoots on the other hand retain a large area from which evaporation does take place in the winter, and the most harmful effect is brought about by bright sunshine following a hard frost, when evaporation goes on with great rapidity and without any possibility of replenishment from the still frozen soil.

A reduction in the rate of evaporation can be brought about by spraying the plant with cold water which will check harmful results of sudden thaws, but more generally it is better to locate such plants out of the range of bright winter sunshine, notably upon a north slope. In such a way it is possible to grow oranges in certain selected sites in the south-western corner of England, with some success if little profit.

## Chapter Four

### OF THE SOIL

"Next came an angry voice—the Rabbit's, 'Pat, Pat, where are you?' And then a voice she had never heard before, 'Sure then, I'm here! Digging for apples!'"

LEWIS CARROLL.

IN all books dealing with gardening as an art the question of the composition of soil appears to be very lightly touched upon.

It is essential that the gardener should understand clearly what is meant by soil, and if the explanations given in the following pages appear elementary to the initiated it is because one feels that the adequacy of the soil for the part which it is to play in the life of the garden is of paramount importance.

It would be wise, therefore, for us to go back to the early years of the world's life to examine how the soil became part of the earth's crust, for it is this crust which enables us to live, to feed, and to enjoy the beauty of our garden. As the earth cooled, this outer layer gradually solidified and covered a spheriod with hard rock. At this time it was still too hot to allow the formation of any kind of moisture upon its surface and was probably surrounded by huge masses of steam. As the interior also began to cool, cracking and folding of the crust took place, and gradually with further cooling the surface at last became low enough in temperature to allow the steam to condense and cover it with moisture in the form of water. This would permeate into the cracks previously formed, penetrate to the hotter parts below, and very quickly be turned to steam with a consequent breaking up of the rock formations about it.

As time went on, the continual heating and cooling would have the tendency of breaking the rock into smaller fragments and so a surface was formed which consisted of pieces of rock of varying sizes which formed the base from which the soil

2. Primula Beesiana

eventually was formed. Later on, when the crust became cool enough for the water to freeze, the expansion of the water in still smaller crevices would cause still further fracturing of the rock and bring down the individual pieces to a much smaller size. The action of water on these smaller pieces would still further reduce their size. Numberless pieces would be washed away, salts would be dissolved out and finally the surface layer would be broken down into pieces of such a size that they could be comparable to what we now call silt and clay.

If one examines the soil above a rock structure one will find that the soil crust near the rock itself is generally composed of larger pieces of rock and with masses of soil quite light in colour, whereas as one approaches the top soil it will be found to be darker in colour and composed of smaller particles. Soil consists of an organic part and an inorganic part. We have traced the construction of the inorganic part, but the organic constituents have been added by the growth and decay of the many billions of living things which have peopled the soil from the earliest time. It is necessary that the organic constituents shall be broken down to simple compounds in order that plants may be able to live upon them. To do this work approximately three thousand millions of tiny plants play their part in each gramme of soil. In addition to these about 750,000 rather larger micro-organisms also live in each gramme of soil. The smaller plants are known as bacteria; the larger organisms are called protozoa. The relation between these is rather like that between the cow and the grass, the bacteria being the grass and the protozoa the cow. Thus it can be seen that if either of these is beneficial to the growth of plant life one should endeavour to ensure their well-being.

The bacteria perform the work of preparing the nitrogen in the air in a suitable form to encourage the growth of plant life, and it is therefore essential that the well-being of the bacteria in the soil should be adequately protected. For this reason it is necessary to consider how these tiny plants live. They require for their well-being that the soil in which they live shall be well-aerated since they cannot exist in soil which is waterlogged, and it is therefore essential that the land should be well drained. It is also found that they do not exist in soils which are too greatly acid, and for this reason the soil should not be allowed to become sour. These are two good reasons for what is called "good cultivation."

So far we have only considered the bacteria which produce the nitrogenous compounds useful in the life of the plant. In addition the plant requires certain mineral salts which are obtained from the inorganic part of the soil. It can be readily seen that since the root of the plant acts, as it were, as its mouth by which it feeds, the particles of the soil which really prove of use to the plant are those which are either very tiny or very soluble. Consequently it is obvious that the part of the soil which is most useful to the plant is that composed of the finest particles, and we must therefore return to an examination of the physical properties of the soil itself.

The division between the stones and sand, sand and silt, and silt and clay is purely an arbitrary one. For instance, it is possible that sand at the larger end of its range may approach what we may call stones; at the smaller end of its range it approaches silt. Silt may be said to be those particles of the soil which range midway between sand and clay, and it therefore is very variable in the size of its individual component particles.

Clay consists of the very finest particles of the soil and provides all the inorganic constituents necessary for the growth of the plant contained in the soil itself.

A good garden soil is said to consist of loam; loam is a natural mixture of clay and silt, and humus and sand, and can therefore be extremely variable in its composition. Sometimes when the clay content is high it is said to be heavy; when the sand content is high it is said to be light, but it should always contain sufficient clay to provide the mineral salts necessary to the life of the plant. In addition to loam, certain other soils can be of use in the garden and it is wise that we consider them at this stage.

It has been mentioned that the organic part of the soil consists of the decaying vegetable matter which had once grown upon its surface. Soils containing a very large percentage of such organic matter are leafmoulds and peats. These consist mainly of organic matter. In the case of peat it is organic matter in a state of arrested decay. This is caused generally by the flooding of the peat and the exclusion of air. By this means it prevents the bacteria from breaking the peat down as they would do in the case of leaf mould.

In order that plants may grow in any kind of soil it is necessary that in addition to the organic and inorganic parts of the soil there shall also be present both air and water, and one must consider the reasons why these two substances occur variably in different types of soils. Water as far as the soil is concerned is only useful when it adheres to the particles of soil in the form of a thin film. It can be readily seen that if the particles of the soil are large, the surface area of each particle compared with its weight is small, as against the surface area of a very large number of tiny particles making up the same weight. As water adheres to the surface of the particles, the large number of tiny particles will therefore hold a great deal more water than a small number of larger particles.

This explains why clay retains a good deal of moisture and why clay soils are said to be heavy. When it is desired to drain soils composed of predominating proportions of clay, lime is added to the soil. This is said to flocculate it and causes the tiny particles of clay to join together as rather larger particles. Thus water is released and is allowed to drain away, with a consequent improvement in the draining capacity of the clay.

The ideal soil consists of clay, humus, silt and sand perfectly balanced, but it is idle, when one is dealing with a piece of land, with the character of soil already fixed, to wish for the ideal. One can, of course, lighten heavy soils, drain waterlogged ones, add lime to sour soils, add humus to worked-out soils; in fact do all these things where they are necessary. But the mere mechanics of gardening should not allow one to suppose that even with a perfect soil one can produce a perfect garden.

Mention has been made earlier of bacteria and protozoa. Many years ago it was noticed that certain soils after a time became what was called "sick" and for no apparent reason crops did extremely badly in these soils. It was because the bacteria were gradually becoming less and less numerous owing to the action of the protozoa which were devouring the bacteria in large quantities, thus depriving plants growing in the soil of their full complement of nitrates. It was found that if the soil was heated to a temperature just below that of boiling water for a period of roughly twenty minutes, the soil regained its former health. The reason for this is quite easy to discover. Protozoa, which closely resemble animals or insects, are killed at this temperature. Bacteria are also killed but leave behind them spores or seeds which are not affected by the heat. Immediately after cooling, the spores begin to grow and to produce further bacteria which, now deprived of their enemies, are able to increase at a phenomenal rate, and soon the soil returns to its former efficiency. The process of heating the soil for this purpose is known as 'sterilisation.' It should, however, be pointed out that this term usually indicates the extermination of all living things, including spores, but as applied to soil it is modified in the sense indicated.

The soil is, of course, of such great importance that each gardener should make a resolution to give as much attention and spend as much money each year upon the well-being of his soil as he does upon plants and seed and labour. So highly did the French peasant care for his soil at the end of the nineteenth century that quite often when he moved he carried the soil with him in as many wagons as he could beg or borrow. The fact that he omitted to steal any was only indicative of the fact that he wished to stay with the soil and not be parted from it.

Quite often I have known people to spend very large sums of money upon plants which they knew they could not grow satisfactorily in the soil of their particular gardens. They have asked advice; they have been given advice; generally the advice was to pay as much attention to the soil as they had done to the acquisition of the plants, i.e., to get the right soil as well as the right plant. Not infrequently they have done so, but on almost every occasion only as an after-thought when everything else had failed.

The analysis of the materials which build up the plant and which are acquired from the air and the soil shows that the plant uses nitrogen, phosphorus, sulphur, potassium, calcium and magnesium in quite considerable quantities. It also uses iron, manganese, sodium, chlorine and silicon in smaller

3. Laburnum Adamii

quantities, and very minute quantities of copper, zinc and other trace elements. It is quite possible that some of these items may not be essential to the plant even though they are contained in it, but the fact remains that they are acquired in the course of its life. The plant also acquires hydrogen and oxygen in the form of water taken up by the roots, and carbon from the air by photosynthesis. These then are the chemical compounds which form the food of the plant.

With the exception of carbon, which is obtained by the action of the green leaves in conjunction with the carbon dioxide which is always present in the air, all the other elements come from the soil. Most of it, however, is not available to the plant because though it is present in the soil for the ready absorption by the plant, it must also be soluble. Moreover these elements must be present in the soil in a nicely balanced proportion, an over-abundance of one element not compensating for the lack of another. For example, chlorosis, that is the yellowing of the leaves of certain plants, is caused by the presence of too much calcium in the soil, but it is not because the plant absorbs too much calcium which causes the yellowing of the leaves, but because the presence of so much of it prevents the plant from absorbing the iron necessary for the production of chlorophyll in its green leaves. The absence of the green colouring prevents the plant from obtaining the necessary carbon from the air, and by a process comparable with starvation the plant begins to wither and to die.

Of all the plant foods nitrogen, phosphorus and potassium are probably the most important. Nitrogen causes the leaves to be of a good bright green, encourages rapid growth and is most in demand while the plant is growing. Too much darkens the colour of the foliage, produces soft growth, delays flowering, reduces resistance to cold and leads to poor quality in flowers and fruits. Phosphorus is specially necessary for growth in the early stages from seed, and for promoting the development of good fruit. It increases the resistance of the plant to cold and disease. It helps to reduce the effects of an excess of nitrogen. Absence or partial absence of phosphorus results in a slowing down of the growth of the plant. Potassium is very important for building up the carbohydrates and fibrous tissues in the plant. It promotes sturdy growth and improves the quality of fruit, increases the plant's resistance to cold, disease and drought. Deficiency leads to stunted growth and mottling of the older leaves. Potassium and nitrogen appear to be complementary in their action, each enabling the plant to make a better use of the other.

The other elements necessary for the well-being of the plant are present in appropriate quantities in almost every soil with perhaps the exception of calcium. This particular constituent prevents sourness of the soil and helps to make available the phosphorus already present in the soil for the benefit of the plant. While it is not part of our object to stress the importance of the conservation of phosphorus in a world which is quickly becoming deficient in this all-important element, it should be pointed out that very steadily the available quantity is being reduced and that until legislation makes it impossible for large quantities of phosphates to be foolishly disposed of, the quantity will be still further diminished to the detriment of the human race.

The amateur who is interested can find that a great deal of instructive information can be gained by growing plants by what is known as the "soil-less method." Here one takes as one's basic material a quantity of clean crushed coke. The plant to be grown is placed in a pot, after the root has been washed entirely clear of all soil, and completely surrounded with a quantity of crushed coke. The pot is then stood in an earthenware saucer into which is poured the following solution:

Dissolve in rain water:
$1\frac{1}{4}$ teaspoonsful Acid Potassium Phosphate, $KH_2PO_4$
4 teaspoonsful Calcium Nitrate Crystals, $Ca(NO_3)_2$ $4H_2O$
$2\frac{1}{2}$ teaspoonsful Magnesium Sulphate, $MgSO_4$ $7H_2O$
$\frac{1}{2}$ teaspoonsful Sulphate of Ammonia, $(NH_4)_2$ $SO_4$
$1\frac{1}{2}$ teaspoonsful Sulphate of Potash, $K_2$ $SO_4$

Make up solution to five gallons.
To each 5 gallons add 2 teaspoonsful of Solution A and 20 teaspoonsful of Solution B.

SOLUTION A. This contains the trace elements necessary for

the proper growth of the plant, corresponding to the essential vitamins for animals.

In ½ gallon of rainwater dissolve 1 teaspoonful each of Boracic Acid, Magnesium Sulphate and Zinc Sulphate, and add ⅛ teaspoonful of Copper Sulphate.

SOLUTION B. Dissolve ¼ teaspoonful of Ferric Chloride ($FeCl_3$) in 1 pint of water.

It will be found that by omitting certain of the elements in the case of other similar plants the comparative value of the various chemical constituents can be measured, and that very little variation in the standard solution quickly demonstrates that lack of balance in the solution leads to abnormal growth in the plant.

An illustration of the importance of the trace elements may be found in certain experiments carried out in America with Ammonium molybdenate in connection with the production of Lettuces. The soil was treated with this chemical at the rate of 250 grains (that is a fraction over ½ ounce) per acre, with remarkable results upon growth. Such a minute proportion indicates how finely balanced a mechanism the soil may become.

But with all this discussion of the physical components of the soil we have not yet considered why it is necessary to cultivate the soil in order that a plant may grow effectively. Cultivation has many and far-reaching results in addition to the destruction of weeds and the facilities it gives for easy planting. If deep enough, it provides good roothold for plants with large root systems. It extends the feeding area of each individual plant and renders more nutritive soil available.

In the past, surface tillage has been held to conserve moisture because it was said to break the continuity of the water skin which surrounded the tiny particles of soil and prevented evaporation in hot dry weather. Recent investigation suggests that it is certain that the plants growing in the soil transpire the moisture through their leaves long before it reaches the upper layers of the soil by means of capillary attraction, so that hoeing, for this reason, cannot be said to conserve moisture in the soil. It is estimated, however, that an average-sized cabbage uses during the course of its lifetime forty gallons of water in order to produce its full growth. From this a parallel may be drawn as to the quantity of water required to support life in each weed growing upon the surface of the garden, each requiring a minimum about two hundred times its own weight during the normal life of the weed. Hoeing, therefore, to eliminate weeds may be said to conserve the moisture in the soil, but for this reason and this reason alone; if weeds can be eliminated by any other means, the necessity for hoeing ceases immediately.

Certain experiments carried out in connection with the growing of cotton deserve quite a little attention. In these the surface of the fields was completely covered with concrete in which quite small apertures were made in which the cotton was grown. The crop proved a complete success, it was free from disease and pests, there were no weeds to compete, no hoeing was necessary and the plants suffered in no way from the drought which affected the surrounding crops. While one cannot draw any certain conclusion from such a venture it does provide food for thought, and when one compares the ability of certain plants to flourish in minute crevices, upon a complete minimum of aerated soil, it does suggest to one's mind that in the science of gardening one cannot afford to be dogmatic about anything, but to approach the subject with a certain humility which should grow greater with the passage of one's years.

It should not be supposed, therefore, that it is necessary to dig in order to cultivate successfully every plant. In the case, for instance, of the Brassicas, that is the cabbages, brussels sprouts and allied plants, it is far better to plant in firm undug ground provided, of course, that it is free of weed, and to feed the plant with artificial fertilisers. Under these circumstances the Brassicas will flourish, whereas if planted in a soil too deeply dug they are likely to take long to establish and consequently prove of insufficient growth.

Still talking of soils, we come to the compost heap. The compost heap can be of extraordinary value to the gardener because it is here that the waste products of the garden can be converted into suitable fertilisers to aid future growth.

The followers of Rudolph Steiner have a peculiar method of preparing their composts which smacks somewhat of witchcraft. In fact it reminds one of the witch's brew so adequately described in *Macbeth*, reversed:

> "Fillet of fenny snake
> In the cauldron boil and bake.
> Eye of newt and toe of frog,
> Wool of bat and tongue of dog,
> Adder's fork and blindworm's sting,
> Lizard's leg and owlet's wing,
> For a charm of powerful trouble
> Like a Hell broth boil and bubble."

Steiner's disciples swear by the results they obtain from their peculiar infusion, but there is no confirmatory evidence which shows that these results are better than those which can be obtained by employing more science and less mystery.

The usual method for making a compost heap is to take the garden refuse and spread it over the surface of the ground to a depth of from six to eight inches. The more the material can be bruised the better. The stalks of such things as cabbages should be crushed. Material like waste paper may be added to a total depth of say six inches. This accumulation should be trampled down and wetted. Over the surface one dusts ¾ oz. of sulphate of ammonia, ½ oz. of superphosphate of lime, 1 oz. of powdered chalk to each square yard. The whole should then be covered with two to three inches of soil and a further layer of vegetable matter added, together with the necessary chemicals and so on until a many-layered sandwich is built up to a height of say three to four feet. Soon the heap will begin to heat up, and if it is then turned the product will be more homogeneous than if it is left alone, though this part of the process is not actually necessary.

It is possible that the more conservative gardener may look askance at the suggestion of incorporating waste damaged paper in the compost heap. I emphasize, however, its immense value by means of a story which I know to be true. Visitors to Southport have no doubt noticed the magnificent tulips grown in the

Promenade Gardens in May. That eminent gardener, Mr. T. Clark, was once asked how he managed to produce such wonderful blooms in a place where it was obvious that the soil was so light as to require constant feeding. His answer consisted of two words only: "Tram tickets." The stupefaction pictured on the face of his listeners was to some degree assuaged when he explained that the waste tram tickets collected in the town were systematically dug into the ground each year to provide a humus content and a medium which would conserve moisture and prevent the quick dissipation of the added fertilisers.

A more modern method of composting and one which has very good results is to build in exactly the same way but to water each successive layer with a solution of potassium permanganate at the rate of ½ oz. to one gallon of water, and one gallon of water to each two square yards. In about three months the material is ready for use, and is just as valuable to the gardener as any kind of farmyard manure.

I cannot stress too strongly the importance of every gardener building his own compost heap and returning to the soil in some form the waste products which have been taken from it. There is an old saying: "You cannot get blood out of a stone." It is equally true that you cannot take out of the garden indefinitely what you are not prepared to replace.

# Chapter Five

## OF THE SEED

"It'll be no use their putting their heads down and saying. 'Come up, dear' I shall only look up and say, "Who am I then? Tell me that first, and then, if I like being that person, I'll come up; if not, I'll stay down here till I'm somebody else! but . . . I do wish they would put their heads down! I am so very tired of being all alone down here."

LEWIS CARROLL.

THE life cycle of the plant begins and ends in the seed. The seed itself is probably the most fascinating of all the phases of plant life. It contains in embryo the plant of a tree which is to provide us with utility or beauty, or a combination of both, but we must think a little more of the seed since it is to provide us in the main with all the many dwellers in our gardens and our woods, our fields and our forests.

The seed of every plant is produced with the express purpose of ensuring that the species shall continue to exist. Often a weakly plant will put forth a last dying effort ; produce an astonishing number of flowers, continue to hang on to life until the seed pods are formed and ripened, and then collapse and die, having accomplished its purpose. Thus it is not always the most healthy plant which produces the best and most fertile seed. The seed is produced as a means to an end: that the species shall not end. In order that the species shall continue the seed varies its characteristics. Some seeds will germinate quickly and readily, others will take some time before actually breaking into growth. In many cases the period is about a year. This is done in order that the seed, which would normally germinate during the following season, should have behind it as a kind of insurance a small number of seeds which would take their place in the event of there being a bad season.

Many seeds have curious idiosyncrasies. For instance, *Canna indica* seeds are, when ripened, as hard as iron; in fact the seed

43

was originally called Indian Shot. Often with old seeds it is wise to soak them in boiling water for some time before sowing and to notch the hard covering of each seed before it is sown. It is said that the seed of *Daphne Mezerum* will germinate during the year of sowing if it is divested of its fleshy outer covering, whereas if it is sown with the fleshy covering still upon it, it will remain dormant for a whole season before showing any signs of germination. Paeonies also have curious seeds. They are best if bedded in the soil deeply for a year and then sown nearer the surface of the ground. If sown in the ordinary way, a few will germinate during the first year of sowing, but the bulk will not make their appearance until over a year has elapsed from the date of the original sowing. Thus it can be seen from the few examples quoted that a study of the seed is nearly as important as a study of the soil, and we shall continue to consider its importance from the point of view of its progeny.

The material which comprises the actively growing green plant contains over 90 per cent of water in its composition. The seed, however, contains only about one-tenth of this proportion of water, so that absorption of water by the seed must precede any germination. For this reason the gardener soaks some of the larger seeds in water before he sows them. The rate of chemical change in the plant depends, within limits, upon the temperature, such chemical changes taking place at a greater rate when the temperature is higher than when it is low. Consequently for this reason the gardener germinates many of his seeds in heat.

While the seeds are still dormant, they may often be encouraged to germinate by being subjected to some variations of temperature. This need occasion little surprise, since day and night temperatures throughout the world are subject to great variation and the seed of the plant is specifically designed to succeed under what would be its normal natural condition. After the seeds have germinated, however, a constant temperature seems to be the desideratum.

A certain measure of stimulation in the germination of some seeds can be brought about by the incorporation of a small quantity of superphosphate of lime in the soil in which they are sown.

4. Cymbidium Lowii var. grandiflorum, a green orchid of appealing charm

A treatment (known as vernalisation) for certain seeds which are not required to be sown immediately is of great interest, for seeds so treated produce plants which develop and mature earlier than those from seeds not so treated, and are indifferent to altered hours of daylight. (See Chapter 8). The method used is to soak the seed in water and then subject it to a constant low temperature of approximately a degree or so below freezing-point for a period of about fourteen days. After treatment the seed may be dried and stored and will upon germination develop as stated. Quite often the progeny can be affected by the treatment of the seed. In some cases it is definitely proved that by the application of certain chemicals to the seed it can be induced to germinate more quickly. Where, for instance, seed is soaked in colchicine it engenders in the next generation a series of freaks which may have the characteristics of giants or dwarfs, and give rise to varieties with large flowers or with contorted or congested growth. Of this we shall write more later.

Some seeds prove of exceptional difficulty to germinate, especially if they are of any great age. Thus the seed of the Pasque flower (*Anemone Pulsatilla*) germinates with great freedom if sown as soon as it is ripe. If, however, it is stored for a month or so, germination is uneven and often does not take place until the following spring. This is equally true of certain kinds of Gentians. It is even recorded that in one particular case storing seed in a waistcoat pocket for some months caused it to germinate with great freedom when sown, after everything else had failed. This is not a practice the author would recommend, since it would probably lead to some congestion in waistcoat pockets. Some seeds require to be frozen before they will germinate with freedom. This is particularly true of some of the wild and alpine plants. It is especially noticeable that if seed boxes of such sowings are placed out in frosty weather and are allowed to become frozen hard and then removed to warmer surroundings, germination takes place almost immediately, and the writer has practised this quite often by placing certain of his seeds before sowing in a refrigerator to make sure that they were well and truly frozen.

Some seeds, and one which springs to mind is *Primula*

*Littoniana*, are light-sensitive, that is they do not germinate readily in the dark. On the other hand, the majority of seeds are not light-sensitive and germinate with much more freedom if light is excluded after they are sown. Some seeds are better if sown while they are still green; an example of this is *Primula Winteri* which undoubtedly grows much more easily if collected while the seed pod is still green and the seeds inside are not too hard. Thus it can be seen that the study of the seed will repay its time in terms of better and more efficient production.

Another seed which germinates most readily when still incompletely ripe is that of the ordinary tomato. If the seed from a half ripe fruit is sown immediately, germination will be found to take place in a remarkably short time, and although the tomato may be said to be exceptionally easy to grow from seed, it will be found that the method suggested gives results which are far better than those obtained from seeds which have been unduly dried.

You will find on reading your gardening encyclopædia that the general rule for sowing seed, especially the seeds of flowers, is to sow as soon as ripe. This may be taken as a good general rule since Nature distributes its seed as soon as it is ripe into the correct surroundings for its proper growth. On the other hand, Nature is extremely prodigal with its seed. Many plants are almost prolific in the production of their seeds as the Starfish in the production of its young; but owing to the fact that the distribution of the seed must be made in the immediate surroundings of the parent plant or be dependent upon external agencies, many of the seeds do not arrive in places where they can grow adequately. The wild Geranium, for instance, distributes its seeds by means of a kind of spring. If you look at the Cranesbill, you will find that its seed pod consists of a long pointed capsule with five rounded protuberances at the base. When the seed is ripe the seed capsule splits at the base and the five sections of the seed pod spring outwards, flinging the seed quite a long distance around. This is particularly annoying to the gardener who wishes to collect the seed, and the only effective way I have ever discovered of doing this is to surround the whole plant with a tube of brown paper. Generally of at least a foot in diameter, this has the effect of confining the seed to an

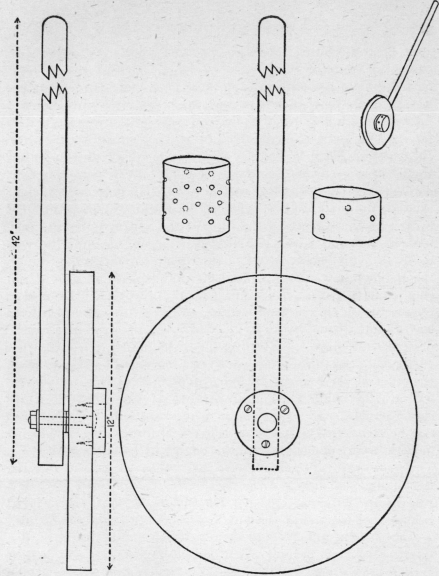

This home-made seed-sower can be of great assistance to the amateur for sowing vegetable seeds.

The materials are a broomstick, a 2½-in. bolt and nut with three washers, three ¾-in. screws, a one-foot disc of hardwood 1 in. thick, and several cutter top tobacco tins. One lid with its rim slit by three cuts forms the holder for the interchangeable cups, which are drilled with holes of various sizes at regular intervals.

For seeds to be sown 3-in. apart, 12 holes are drilled at equal distances round one of the tins; 4-in. apart, 9 holes; 6-in. apart, 6 holes; 8-in., 7 holes; 9-in., 4 holes; 1 ft., 3 holes. The size of the hole should be determined by the size of the seeds. Where patch sowing is required the hole should be made large enough to drop three or four seeds from each hole. Where a seed bed for cabbage is being sown a deeper tin with approximately 72 holes evenly distributed over the cylindrical surface in three distinct rows is needed.

The method of use comprises making a drill, filling the right cup with the appropriate seed, clipping it into place in the lid, and gently wheeling the machine along the drill.

area of something less than a square foot, and renders its collection comparatively easy.

In addition to being sown at the correct time, the seed should be, as far as the gardener is concerned, correctly sown. Here I find without a doubt that as far as flower seeds are concerned by far the best results are obtained by sowing in sterilised soil on the lines described in Chapter 3, and covering the surface, after the seed has been sown, with coarse grit of about $\frac{1}{8}$″ in diameter. This renders it difficult for such things as moss and various types of fungi to find the necessary foothold. Germinations are even, and the surface of the soil is sufficiently well ventilated, but yet not too well ventilated to become dry. In this way many difficult plants can be raised without undue precautions.

Of sowing in the garden itself one should be certain that conditions at the time that this is done are suitable. It is useless to sow in soil that is waterlogged, and as a rule just as futile to sow in soil that is too dry. The right kind of friability can be determined by carefully feeling the soil.

In many cases the man who sows his vegetable seeds makes the mistake of sowing far too thickly. A rather neat device for sowing such seeds is illustrated in this chapter. It is easy to make, and by means of interchangeable cups the seed can be sown in batches and reduces thinning after sowing. I have on many occasions used this device with admirable results. The great thing to remember is to change the cup to suit the size of seed which is to be sown. Seeds that are badly sown as a rule in the vegetable garden are the edible peas. Here I am certain that in spite of the time taken being greater than for an ordinary sowing, the results are so much·better that it is well worth doing properly. When sowing a number of rows of garden peas, prepare a strip of ground for each row a foot wide and plant the seeds individually in four rows three inches apart, each seed being three inches from the one before it. Thus the total number of seeds required for a fifty foot row is approximately eight hundred. You will find with this type of sowing that the haulms are strong and healthy, the spacing being ample to provide adequate ventilation. It is quite certain that anything which the gardener does to sow the seed a little thinner amply repays the pains taken.

5.  A carefully sited Oak, planted by a visionary

Certain seeds which are very tiny are better mixed with five or six times the quantity of fine sand to aid in even distribution. Others, which are difficult to sow because they are nearly the colour of the soil, are better if dusted with a little flour. This helps them to show up when they are sown. Those appreciated by mice are better soaked in either paraffin or rolled in red lead. in the case of the former, mice are said to dislike the smell; in the second case the compound would seem to be added as a wild kind of justice to impede the digestion. Of the two practices I think the first is preferable. One of the things which appears to discourage mice is the presence of fresh mint. This I have tried on many occasions and found to be completely adequate in preventing their depredations.

It would be as well to summarise for the gardener some of the points which he should bear in mind when obtaining seeds. First of all the seed should always be fresh. As a rule the seed of flowering plants can be safely collected within the confines of his own garden, always provided that he does not require them to be of particularly pure breeding. He can collect without trouble the seeds of mostly all of the herbaceous plants from the border. He can collect the seed of practically all the plants in the rock garden. It does not follow, however, that when they are sown they will be of either the same colour or characteristics of their parents since cross pollination can have taken place, and the strain need no longer be true. In the case of vegetables the same thing may equally apply. Without going deeply into the question of Mendelism, at this stage it is enough to say that hybridisation will also take place in the majority of the varieties grown in the vegetable garden. This, however, does not mean that the grower who wishes to save the seed of a particularly good tomato plant does not stand a very good chance of obtaining from his seeds, plants of equal merit. What is certain, however, is that it is not likely that every seed will produce a plant of equal merit. Thus the gardener can save the seed of outstandingly good plants, but he should only select the seed from such plants and should continue each year only to save the best.

Seed which is old, it has been pointed out, germinates unevenly and should be avoided. The seed of plants subject to disease should not be saved, but within these limits the gardener may do much to provide for himself. The seedsman, however, is particularly useful for providing seeds of even performance since his seed is produced under circumstances where hybridisation would be the exception and not the rule; he spends a great deal of time and money on the production of improved varieties, and does in fact on a very much larger scale what the gardener who saves his own seed does. He selects and re-selects, always with the object of getting something better and more useful, and since he grows more he can select and re-select in much shorter time, and can produce in large quantities any of the new varieties which he feels the public will demand. The gardener, therefore, must use the seedsman to provide the new varieties which he requiries to stock his garden, to provide also those things which he cannot produce himself and, in addition, to provide the seeds which he has failed to produce himself, and finally, to provide those seeds to replace varieties which he considers are no longer worth growing.

While we talk of seeds it might be well to touch upon what is known as the genetic constitution, or, in other words, their hereditary characteristics. If we consider a plant like the Dahlia, which is of comparatively recent introduction into horticulture, we shall see that there are an extremely large number of garden varieties of all shades of colour, size, and shape. Actually the original Dahlia, *Dahlia variabilis*, which came from Mexico in 1789, was a single-flowered variety with a yellow centre and dull red petals, and in 1879 came *Dahlia Juarezii*, the forerunner of the cactus Dahlia, which was also crimson in colour. How then have these varieties been evolved? For this purpose it would be well to consider an experiment which was made with the red-flowered and white-flowered varieties of an American plant named *Mirabilis jalapa*, or more simply Four o'clock or Marvel of Peru. The pollen from the white-flowered variety was used to fertilise the ovaries of the red-flowered variety and vice versa. The resultant seed was sown; the plants were all discovered to have pink flowers, irrespective of the fact that the male or female parent had white or red flowers. When, however, the pollen of these plants was used to fertilise the ovaries of the same plant and the resultant seed was sown, some of the new plants had white flowers, some had red, and some had pink.

To what can we ascribe this peculiar happening? The simplest explanation is that a particle of living matter is transmitted from the parent to the offspring which determines or helps to determine the flower colour in the succeeding generation. This living particle is known as the "gene." The red-flowered plant contributes what we call a red gene, the white-flowered plant a white gene. For the sake of simplicity we will call these R for the red gene, and r for the white gene. The offspring, therefore, has one of each kind, and so the resultant generation will have one gene which influences a red colour, and one which will influence a white colour, with the result that the flowers are pink. The genes, however, do not mix but remain quite distinct. When the time comes for them to form new male or female cells for reproduction, they separate so that each pollen grain will have either R or r, and the ovary will have either R or r. Hence there is an equal chance for either kind of ovary to be fertilised by either kind of pollen grain. If an R pollen grain fertilises an R ovary, it gives us the combination of RR. If, however, it fertilises an r ovary, we shall have Rr. In a similar way an r pollen grain will fertilise either an R or r ovary, giving us Rr or rr.

From this it is easy to see that if we strike an average of the second generation, one quarter will be of the denomination RR. One half will be of the denomination Rr, and one quarter will be of the denomination rr. But it is obvious that since R disposes towards a red colouring, the denominations RR will have red flowers; the denomination Rr will have pink flowers, and the denomination rr will have white flowers. In this case the more powerful gene is said to be dominant; the weaker gene is said to be recessive, but it still remains, and at some future period it may disclose its presence by producing among the descendants a number of offspring of the original recessive type.

So far we have only considered what happens in the case of one characteristic. The Abbe Mendel of Austria conducted a series of experiments in the middle of the nineteenth century upon which all our present knowledge of genetics has been based. The experiments dealt with garden peas. He found that the yellow and green colour of peas were inherited in the same way that colour in the flower is inherited. Some peas are rounded and smooth, others are wrinkled. This difference is due to another pair of genes, round being dominant to wrinkled. The question arises as to what would happen if both sets of characters were employed in a cross. What would happen, for instance, if a plant which has green, round peas in its pods, were crossed with a variety with yellow and wrinkled seeds in its pods? From what we know of the experiment with Mirabilis we can deduce what is likely to happen. We will use Y for the gene producing yellow colour, y for the gene producing the green colour, R for the gene that produces round seeds, and r for the gene responsible for the wrinkles.

The original plants could therefore be denoted by the symbols yy RR and YY rr. Let us suppose that the pollen was taken from the first plant, namely the plant denoted by the symbols yy RR. Each grain of pollen can only contain one y and one R, whereas the ovaries of the other plant contain one Y and one r when the fertilisation actually took place. The new seeds would have the character Yy Rr, which gives us the genetic constitution of the seeds of the first generation, but Y is dominant to y, so all peas will be yellow, and R is dominant to r, so all the peas will be round. If, however, these peas are now sown, they will grow up and produce both pollen and ovaries in which only one of each pair of genes will be found. One half will contain Y; one half will contain y, and the other half R and the last half r; but as the separation of Y from y is nothing to do with the separation of R and r, one half of the pollen grains with Y will contain R and the other half r. Thus both the ovaries and the pollen grains will contain the genes paired in four different ways:

YR    yR
Yr    yr

Which kind of pollen grain will fertilise any kind of ovary is a matter of chance, but it must be apparent that four different types of peas will be produced,—round green peas, wrinkled yellow peas, like the original generation, yellow round peas like the first generation, and an altogether new type with wrinkled green peas. It must also be apparent that some of each of these types will be able to breed true if crossed with varieties similar to themselves. For instance, peas of the genetic constitution YY RR will breed true for yellowness and roundness quite unlike those of the first generation, which look like them but have the genetic constitution Yy Rr. The new type of peas yy rr will also breed true, and give green wrinkled peas. No new genes have been formed, a regrouping only has taken place. This regrouping is known as re-combination and it is this re-combination which enables new varieties to be produced. Taken as a group on an average it will be seen that there are four true breeding groups in the 16 evolved from such a combination, so that on the average only one plant exhibiting the new characteristics will be found in every 16. This of course only applies to plants in which it is desired to re-combine two pairs of genes; it must be obvious that if three pairs of genes are to be re-combined the number of plants from which one of the new type can be chosen will be much greater, a true-breeding new type of given characteristics being evolved in this case only on the average of one in every sixty-four. This, it should be understood, is merely an attempt to explain simply the laws governing the genetics of plants, and though a number of exceptions and a great many complications intervene in actual practice, the principles remain constant and are used by agriculturists to evolve new plants, and to improve upon the older ones.

Cultivation in itself can improve plants normally growing wild, in the same way that the carrot has been improved by cultivation. Selection of seed has led to further improvements, and cross-breeding to still further advancement, in such a way that the ultimate result compares favourably in all respects with the original wilding.

Some mention has been made of the treatment of plants with Colchicine, which is an extract from the bulb of the autumn crocus. A few years ago it was discovered that Colchicine slows down the process of growth in some ways but not in others. It retards the production of cells but allows the chromosomes to continue to be produced at the same rate. The number of chromosomes per cell is thus increased, sometimes doubled and sometimes quadrupled.

Horticulturists have frequently in the past crossed various

plants to obtain hybrids; these are unfortunately often sterile, which reduces their usefulness considerably. This is caused by the fact that the chromosomes do not regroup themselves in the reproductive cells, but when the chromosomes have been doubled each individual chromosome has a mate and pairing is perfectly normal.

Since each chromosome is identical with its mate, the off-spring is uniform. In this way a new strain is obtained much more quickly than when it was dependent upon crossing back or selections. It should not be assumed, however, that Colchicine-treated organisms are always larger and stronger than those of the untreated parent. They may be dwarf or badly formed. Selection can then be made to reject the monstrosities and re-select the useful varities.

In the early experimental stages giant forms could be produced only in the second generation, but more recent investigation has shown that certain seeds which have been soaked in a solution of Colchicine of 1/200,000, can be induced to produce giantism in the same generation. The average amateur will however have to await the availability of Colchicine, the whole output of which is at present absorbed for medical purposes.

## Chapter Six

### OF PLANTING

" 'Why' said the Dodo, 'the best way to explain it is to do it.'
(And, as you might like to try the thing yourself some
winter day, I will tell you how the Dodo managed it.)"

LEWIS CARROLL.

YOU may be the lucky possessor of the " green finger," that
is, you may possess the enviable knack of being able to plant
with every success. On the other hand you may be one of
those unfortunate folk who cast the shadow of fatality over everything they plant. I am not sure that this mythical " green finger "
is not responsible for more deaths than indefinite lives. To me
planting is a scientific pursuit. If a plant is correctly planted,
it lives; if it is incorrectly planted, it dies. It is certain that in
order to plant correctly one should know something about the
root system of plants, trees or shrubs. For instance, it is essential
to know whether the tree is deep-rooted or surface-rooted;
whether it is tolerant of lime or intolerant of it; whether it
requires a damp situation or a dry one; whether it requires
shade or the benefit of much sunlight. These are the main
essentials, and the correct answer to each of them will ensure
that the plant has a happy and fruitful life. Let us take these
items in their correct order.

Quite obviously, if one is planting trees or shrubs, one can
see at a glance whether the roots go deeply into the ground, or
whether they spread in a mat along the surface layer of soil.
It should be an axiom to plant trees in a similar fashion to the
way in which they were originally growing. Fortunately, trees
obtained from nurseries or from the wild show a sign on their
trunks of the original depth of their planting, and they should
be planted neither higher nor deeper than the mark upon the
stem shows them to have been previously planted.

Certain trees or shrubs, like Rhododendrons, are definitely

55

surface-rooted, so that the soil in which they grow is only the very topmost layer. It is, therefore, quite unimportant whether the subsoil is composed of any particular divergent material. Forrest tells us that he found Rhododendrons growing in masses of very wet, black peaty soil of no more than three to six inches in depth, immediately superimposed upon limestone. Such a Rhododendron would be completely intolerant of lime, and fortunately its roots never managed to reach the lime.

Certain of the Prunus trees are surface-rooted and provided they are given all they require in the way of nourishment in the top soil, they will remain perfectly happy and grow and flourish to delight the eye until old age at last cuts them off. The rule, therefore, is to plant your tree with intelligence, not with the "green finger."

The other three items outlined are not completely independent of one another. For instance, one may quote as an example *Gentiana sino-ornata*. This wonderful Gentian, which colours the autumn with the blue of the Mediterranean Sea, grows best in a soil composed almost completely of some form of humus, that is, in peatmould or leafmould, especially where it is living in the sun. If one attempts growing it in a soil containing any lime it turns yellow, it lingers, it dies. On the other hand, if one plants it in a damp but shady place where much free lime is present in the soil, it does not turn yellow, it does not wither, and it does not die, but continues to flourish, though not quite so well as in a position where it gets sunshine and grows in leafmould.

It would appear from this that there is a factor which relates the three requirements in such a measure that the needs of the plant are met even when any two of them, taken without the third are fatal to its well-being. It seems to be a good general rule, however, to say that plants which are intolerant of lime in the sun will sometimes be quite tolerant of it in the shade.

The best way in which to learn the actual conditions under which a plant or tree will flourish is to examine the situation in which it is found in a friend's garden. Alternatively, to discover its exact requirements from a sound book, or finally to consider the conditions under which the plant grows best in its natural habitat. I would place these in that order of virtue, as it is not always an easy proposition to encourage a plant existing under a series of conditions to live under similar circumstances in a different country or climate.

This brings me finally to the still vexed question of the "green finger." More plants die every year after planting for one particular reason than for all other reasons combined. This is because they are too lightly planted. If you consider a tree growing in a field, you will realise that the soil into which it is rooted consists of one homogeneous whole. It does not consist of a bowl of lightly compounded soil generally worked in around the roots. Under such conditions the tree would be rooted out of the ground at the merest puff of wind. It would obtain no nourishment and would be destined for the bonfire before many days had elapsed. It is quite easy to see that such a tree planted in such a bowl could only come into the fulness of life if the soil around its root was firmly pressed down so that it became an integral part of the surrounding soil. Thus a further rule for planting makes itself obvious, namely that the plant should be firmly planted, and this is what the gardener means when he says 'tread the soil well in,' and no matter how small or delicate the plant, provided the soil is in good condition for planting, it can only be improved if the soil immediately around it is sufficiently firmed with the pressure of the foot.

And thus to another consideration. When is the soil fit for planting? The answer here is equally obvious to determine. Since we have made it of paramount importance that our plants shall be firmed in with the foot, we can test the suitability of the soil for planting by treading in this way in any part of the garden with similar soil. If by treading upon it firmly we churn it into a mass of mud or into clods of clay which will make very good bricks, it is quite obvious that the soil is definitely unfit. If, on the other hand, the pressure of the foot leaves us with a nice smooth but breakable surface, then we know that the ground itself is eminently suitable for our purpose.

In the case where the trees or shrubs consist of scions of one type of tree grafted on another, or of trees which are budded upon various root stocks, it is wise when planting to cover the point at which the root stock was originally budded. For ordinary planting, as a rule, it is safe to say that most plants are more suitable upon their own roots, with the possible exception of the modern garden varieties of rose, or in trees where very quick development is required. It should be remembered that budding and grafting are employed by the Nurseryman to shorten the production period and so inclines to produce quick growth which can be out of character. This is particularly noticeable in the case of certain of the small Conifers, and one can only hope that in the future these will become available growing upon their own roots, since under these circumstances one can get the neat characteristic growth of the tree rather than the diffuse growth of the graft. It should be remembered that Conifers are mostly Highland plants, but they all do fairly well where the soil is good or rich. There are, however, so many species, and they have such widely divergent characteristics, that the successful grower must note with care their requirements of soil exposure and climate, and once again consult his friends or his library.

I end on a more personal note. The gardener who values his garden and his trees, the gardener who is really attached to his plants and thinks of them as his friends or helpers in a world in which friends and helpers can smooth away the difficulties of life and make it more happy and tolerable, will long to enlarge this happy circle. The man who continues to grow his "old friends" year after year without introducing fresh acquaintances which will ripen into friends, misses one of the greatest attractions of the true gardener. Each year try to introduce into your garden something new, something different from what you have previously grown. Thus one can have variety in a world which sees far too little of this precious anodyne.

As an example of this, you may remember that in 1825 Jean Louis Adam grafted upon a stock of *Laburnum vulgaris* a graft of *Cytisus purpureus*. The resultant tree produces the typical hanging golden racemes of the Laburnum. In addition it produces the whip-like sprays of purplish pink flowers of *Cytisus purpureus,* but apart from these two kinds of flowers it produces a further kind, resembling the drooping sprays of the Laburnum in contour but lacking their size, and showing the most curious shades of apricot and purple. Now *Laburnum Adamii*, as it is called, has been in existence for well over a hundred years, and I have found it only in the gardens of three of my friends. It is particularly easy to grow, particularly beautiful, particularly interesting, and generally absent. (See Plate III).

We can go back even further. The very delightful *Rosa alba*, an outstandingly sweet-scented white rose which makes a delightful hedge or specimen plant in the garden, has been known since the year 1597 and has presumably been grown in gardens from that date onwards, but I cannot find it in the gardens of even three of my friends, though in beauty of line, in the enchanting and lingering fragrance of its flowers, it is outstanding and unforgettable, and yet it remains among those unremembered!

We may go back still further. You will remember the lines "Consider the lilies of the field, they toil not neither do they spin." This is popularly supposed to refer to one of two plants. Some say it refers to *Sternbergia lutea*, commonly known as the Winter Daffodil, which produces large yellow crocus flowers in September or October and provides a delightful counterpart to the Daffodil in autumn. The other possible plant is *Anemone fulgens*, which produces its brilliant red flowers with their black stamens in May and is perfectly placed in the hot dry grass about the bole of a tree; generally a deciduous tree, because it does require a certain amount of moisture at the time when it is breaking into flower, so as to obtain sufficient drink to enable its bulb to survive for yet another season.

These are some of the plants which are old but are still far from receiving the attention they deserve. There are many hundreds of others. There are two plants, however, of recent introduction, which because of their good habit or good colour or outstanding scent should also figure in the modern garden. One which leaps to mind immediately is a relative of the potato, to which, however, it bears not the slightest resemblance since as far as I am aware no part of it is edible. This plant is *Nierembergia caerulea*, which produces masses of violet blue, salver-shaped flowers with yellow eyes upon short bushy plants with fine grassy leaves from May until the frost cuts short its flowering career. Another plant deserving a great deal of attention is *Verbena corymbosa*. It grows to a height of some three or four feet and bears flowers which both in appearance and scent resemble those of the Heliotrope. *Verbena corymbosa* comes from South Africa, but has proved of intense hardness and is decidedly an acquisition for the flowering border. I will suggest, therefore, that every gardener should follow the advice given to the bride: "Something old, something new, something borrowed, something blue."

## Chapter Seven

### OF THINGS GREEN

"'What *can* all this green stuff be ?' said Alice."

"'I can't help it,' said Alice very meekly. 'I'm growing.'
'You've no right to grow here,' said the Dormouse."

LEWIS CARROLL.

PERHAPS the first thing that strikes a visitor from the
Colonies on reaching this country is the greenness of the
grass. I have heard such visitors for the first week or so
after their arrival comment daily upon its brilliance. We
perhaps take it too much for granted, and fail to appreciate
how truly remarkable green can be as a colour.

During the past few years I have had much to do with the
actual photography of plants and trees in colour, and I have
come to the conclusion that there are many thousands of different
shades of green, tending to be yellow at one end of their range
and purple and blue at the other. In the garden it is the association of these peculiar shades of green which can give so much
pleasure, and it is essential in all shrub borders that some attention should be given to the association of the correct kinds of
plants so that the maximum benefit may be obtained from their
colours.

Green is the most adequate colour for the foliage of plants.
It can, however, be disappointing in other ways. I remember
quite well a most hideous carnation of a peculiar shade of green
which was described in my youth as Eau de Nil. This proved a
source of great annoyance to me because I was perfectly certain
in my young mind that the wretched thing had been dyed, and
its effect upon me was to encourage a tendency towards bilious-
ness. Green flowers can, however, be quite attractive. There is
a rose, *Rosa chinensis* variety *viridiflora*, which consists of a considerable number of petals, each exactly like a leaflet with ser-

rated edge in the same way as the rose itself. This, being natural, does not annoy. There are of course other green flowers. Another which I like is the climbing Gentian, *Crawfurdia trinervis*, which is a greenish yellow marked with patches of violet; this can offend no one; in fact it tends only to fascinate. Another plant with a flower which is almost always green is *Celsia bugulifolia*, which has a verbascum flower of dark green, usually marked with buff and violet, which at first looks repellent, but which gradually proves to attract. It exercises the same fascination as an ugly man; at first one merely looks, and then one goes back to look again, and finally one stays to look.

While we still talk of flowers that are green, there is the Orchid, or to give it its correct name the Cymbidium, illustrated in Plate IV. No one can look at this picture and fail to appreciate the fact that to alter the colour of the dorsal petals of this particular flower would entirely spoil its sophisticated beauty. This provides such an adequate contrast to the hideous carnation which sticks in my mind that I choose it as an antidote, and whenever I wish to banish the horror I spend my time regarding this beauty.

But essentially it is not of flowers that we wish to talk. It is of trees and shrubs, grass, and even of green paint. First of all let us keep to grass. It is the habit of my friends to ask my advice. Some years ago one of them, seized with a desire to improve his lawn, asked me what he should use upon it. I told him sulphate of ammonia. He asked me where he could get it. I told him I thought it could be obtained quite cheaply from the local Gas Company. He obtained large quantities of sulphate of ammonia which he applied early one morning to his somewhat dilapidated lawn. Only one day elapsed before the telephone rang with shrill alarm and an irate voice informed me that I had ruined his lawn. I was loath to point out that my gratuitous advice was not complete, so I asked: "Well, what did you do to it?" He told me. I think he had applied sufficient sulphate of ammonia in the form of a powder to cover about one thousand such lawns with good effect. However, it fortunately rained for about ten days with almost unceasing vigour, and chancing to meet him in the street some three or four weeks later I slunk round a hoarding, hoping to avoid what I thought might be an unpleasant meeting, only to be stopped with a shout obviously intended for me. Coming up with a smile he said: "Oh. My lawn." I nodded. "Well," he said, "it has never been better." I was aghast. Actually the treatment should have killed it a dozen times over, but apparently the rain had saved it. After the application of sulphate of ammonia the top became just a mass of dried-up chaff without a green leaf showing anywhere, but with the overdose of the chemical washed away, the roots again sprang into life, and never before had I seen this particular lawn look so green. However, it is not a process I would recommend. The moral of the story is never to do such a job without fully understanding how much of any particular chemical should be applied. In particular, one should seek to get adequate details of the method of application since in many cases chemicals can be applied either wet or dry, and in the event of their being applied in the wrong way the result can be most disastrous.

While one is talking of lawns and of sulphate of ammonia, it is wise, I think, to give the right proportion for a top dressing. The correct method is to add to each bushel of prepared soil two ounces of sulphate of ammonia. This should be worked in to the surface of the lawn with the back of a wooden rake or with a piece of flat board nailed at the end of a broomstick. A spreading movement should be made with this implement to work the fine soil in around the grass. Such a dressing, which is given in the early spring, should have the effect of producing a really good green lawn. Sulphate of ammonia is also used in conjunction with sand as a weed killer in lawns. Here one waits until a shower has damped the surface of the grass and the weeds which we presume infest it, and broadcast over. It will be seen that much more of the material adheres to the wide-leaved plants, and with the killing of the leaves the grass around the wide-leaved weeds is able to take hold and grow before they recover. It is not sufficient, however, to assume that such preparations really eradicate weeds. They discourage them, but they very rarely exterminate them.

A weed, we are told elsewhere, is a plant in the wrong place. This is, of course, a prime truth, but weeds have to be eradicated by methods varying according to their actual location. Where land is not required to be cultivated immediately after being freed from weeds, certainly in not less than six months, sodium chlorate provides perhaps the best medium. This is a solid which, when dissolved in water and sprayed over a patch of weeds, will exterminate them without fail. It has but two drawbacks. The ground remains infertile for about six months after application, and it creeps. Fortunately it is not poisonous either to human beings or to animals, so that it may be applied with perfect safety. It has, however, one danger. It should be kept away from clothing, and also after it had dried one should not walk among the weeds which it has killed. A story will illustrate the reason for this. I did know of one person who spilt a considerable quantity of rather strong sodium chlorate solution over part of his clothes. After a time it dried and left a white deposit on the surface which he tried to rub off, only to find that his clothes caught fire. Hence the warning. Sodium chlorate has another bad habit—it creeps. That is to say that when applied near the edge of a border on a path it can cause the death of plants which are, say, a foot away. It should therefore be used with care as a weed killer in paths, and should not be overapplied, but used rather to eradicate individual weeds. Of other weed killers there are many. They will be found in the Journals of nurserymen and sundriesmen, together with their appropriate method of application. I would stress, however, the fact that weed killers should as far as possible be harmless to birds, since much suffering can be inflicted upon them which can never be seen by human eye. Keep if you can, to weed killers which are completely innocuous to animal life.

Unpleasant green things are weeds, we are told—but is this really so? I know a bed of *Romneya trichocalyx* so thick, so wide, so prolix, that it has evicted all its competitors and taken possession even more completely of it than the Rose Bay Willow Herb, to such an extent that I now regret the hours I once spent trying unsuccessfully to propagate it. I can never forget having once planted for a friend that most delightful of all the Convolvulus family, *Convolvulus althaeoides*, and the subsequent efforts to undo the damage, the patient and untiring work of removing every tiny piece of living root in the top two feet of soil. No, a weed is just a plant growing too quickly where it is

6. Lilium Dalhansonii, a lily of unusual colour

not required, or where it is not subject to adequate competition. Many weeds are intrinsically beautiful and among my favourites I number *Veronica filiformis*, *Hieracium aurantiacum* (Grim the Collier), whose appearance in flower never fails to stimulate my mind and my fingers. Weeds are like their more sedate relatives the plants, both annual, biennial, and perennial, and just as prolific in their production of seeds, though in justice it must be said that some which really produce no fertile seeds can be the most persistent of all.

Some annual weeds such as Chick-Weed, Groundsel, Shepherd's Purse, the red Poppy, and the Plantain, are extremely prolific in the production of their seeds, which retain their vitality so long and so well that land reclaimed from pasture will in its first year give rise to crops of weeds of kinds which have not been seen in that land in living memory.

It is important, therefore, that weeding should be done long before the seed has a chance to mature. As many of the varieties produce several generations of progeny during each year, it is vital that weeding to discourage annual weeds should be done early in the year.

The hairy Cress (*Cardamine hirsuta*) under moist conditions attains a considerable size without producing undue quantities of seed; but let it grow in a dry, light soil, and it produces three to four insignificant leaves and only a few microscopic flowers, but these are succeeded by the typical long seed-pod of the Crucifers, nicely filled with fat seeds, which are flung far and wide when the capsule is agitated by a gentle breeze, or when the eager hand of the gardener approaches to gather them to burn.

Should damp weather conditions ensue at any time, the far-flung seed gives rise to a brood of children, making up a family difficult to control. The fact that the leaves of this pest are edible and vie in flavour with ordinary Watercress is an insufficient inducement to allow it to become an inhabitant of any garden.

But of all weeds the perennial ones are undoubtedly the most difficult to eradicate. The common Bindweed, of which every piece of root is an embryonic new and equally robust plant, almost exceeding the Horseradish in its space-devouring

C.K.                                                                    E characteristics, is extremely difficult to eradicate. The Willow Herb, profuse in its production of aerially prepared seeds, parachuting far and wide, is equally profuse in its production of underground offsets. The creeping Thistle, the Coltsfoot, and the Winter Heliotrope are all greedy gourmands of space, sending out underground shoots not fully appreciated until the extent of their growth becomes obvious in the spring.

Equally devastating, though more obvious in their attacks, are the creeping Buttercup and the Cinquefoil, the Silverweed (*Potentilla Anserina*), *Potentilla reptans*, and *Potentilla fragariastrum*.

I know of no reason why the green flag should be a signal that things are all right. Perhaps it is that the plant signals its well-being by the healthy colour of its foliage. When we meet our friends in the morning we say: "You look well to-day," judging mainly by their appearance. This is equally true of plants. The well-being of a plant can be judged first of all by its foliage, but we do not necessarily grow all our plants for the benefit of their foliage. That is quite true with such things as cabbages and lettuces, which through this medium provide us with much useful food. On the other hand, a plant is designed as a rule to produce its foliage, its flowers, and its fruit in the correct proportion, and so the foliage must be regarded as the outward, visible sign of the adequacy of the plant's food.

You may have a dislike of fat people; you may, on the other hand, feel that they are at least happy; you may also translate this dislike or liking into terms of likes and dislikes in the vegetable kingdom. For instance, I personally do not like big marrows. Why I cannot say. Perhaps it is just an idiosyncrasy. In this liking or disliking of plants one has to bear in mind their actual composition. The plant can be just as gross as an overfed pig. It can produce too much leafage. Earlier we have stated the reason for this overgrowth of green foliage. But disease can also produce a variegation of the foliage; in fact, in some cases the foliage can become almost all white. It is from these things that one gauges the health of the individual plant, and it is from these things that one judges the appropriate treatment.

So in the plant, green is a signal that all is well. Variation of this colour indicates that something has gone wrong, and the good gardener learns at once that his expert attention is required. Quite often the plant will lose its coloration owing to an iron deficiency in the soil. Usually, it is sufficient to water the surrounding soil with a very weak solution of iron sulphate in the proportion of two teaspoonsful to each gallon of water to make it recover its normal bright green coloration.

Of course, this question of the colour of the foliage is one that is subject to a great deal of variation. Just as some particular trees have a very bright and vivid green colouring, others tend to have a colouring which varies towards gold. This can be clearly seen in the case of *Aesculus hippocastanum*, variety *Memmingeri*, which is a very beautiful golden-leaved Horse Chestnut. The contrast between the very dark green of a Yew and the intense gold of the Horse Chestnut is extremely fine, but it would be wrong to assume that because of this variation in colouring one or other was unhealthy. The green colouring of plants or trees can vary amazingly. Similarly the green Beech, the peculiar purple tone of the foliage of *Prunus Pissardii*, together with the contrast of the Cyprus, give three different colour tones, all of which denote abundant health.

Finally in our study of the trees we come to the picture of an Oak. This particular Oak is probably the finest specimen of its kind growing in the South of England. It was planted in the year 1819, is eighty feet high, has a girth of thirty feet, and is in every way a kingly tree. A story is told of a timber merchant walking through the park in which it is situated, looking at it with most admiring and covetous eyes. He went over, passed his hands over the bark, looked the tree up and down, thought it over carefully, pondered it again, and finally was moved by its magnificence to make a remark. At last it came. "Ah," he said, "a beautiful tree. It is worth eighteen Pounds." The value of the story is much greater than that, if only as a warning! (Plate V).

One can get back to the obvious position of the camera when this picture was taken: look up at its great height, see the blue of the sky against its wonderful head and the light of the sun reflected on its foliage and trunk, and think of the day, well over one hundred years ago, when a man with vision caused it to be planted so that you and I and the timber merchant should benefit from its beauty. I am quite sure that on the day on which it was planted no one was thinking of the timber that it might produce in this year of grace. The man who plants trees, and trees of this kind, must have a long vision, and it is only among gardeners that this patience can be found. Let us give thanks at least to the man who planted the Oak so long ago.

And so we come to green paint. This is, of course, a matter of personal taste, but I have never yet found any green paint which bears the slightest resemblance to, or has the ability to make itself at home with, the green of grass, the green of trees or shrubs, or with the green of plants generally. And so I feel that it is unwise to use green paint to any great extent in the garden. On the whole it is my opinion that wood treated with colourless Cuprinol fits much better than wood that has been coloured with paint. Cuprinol has the advantage of being easy to apply. It is clean; it is harmless to plants in the open and it arrests all forms of decay, and is, moreover, a potent fungicide. It can be applied over paint, but painting is completely unessential if woodwork is treated with this compound. I have used it for many years and have never found it to have the slightest drawback other than a rather pungent odour when being applied in a closed shed. In the open it can be applied without the slightest discomfort. If you feel, as I do, on the subject of green paint, you have the choice of two things: either use another and less difficult colour to match, or use some such product as Cuprinol, where the natural colour of the wood can be retained and will weather with age to fit in its surroundings.

# Chapter Eight

## OF LIGHT AND HEAT

" 'You mean you can't take less,' said the Hatter; 'It's very easy to take more than nothing.'"

LEWIS CARROLL.

THE great influence of sunlight upon plants has been earlier indicated in the references to photosynthesis, but it is not only in this way that sunlight affects the growing plants. The anecdote of the plant—generally a sunflower—to add point to the story—which turns its flowers to follow the sun throughout the day, only eventually to twist off its own head, has a basis of truth even if the denouement is ludicrous.

The green plant is in itself a complete demonstration of the scientific principle known as the conservation of energy. The source of its energy is the sunlight which falls upon it, which enables it to combine the carbon dioxide which it inspires with the water it has absorbed from the soil, thus to form sugar. It is estimated that the absorbed energy needed to produce 1 lb of sugar in the growing plant is that required to raise the temperature of four gallons of ice-cold water to the boil, and if the sugar thus produced is but efficiently burnt without loss it would give rise to precisely this amount of heat, and the products of its burning would comprise the same quantities of carbon dioxide and water as were originally combined to produce it.

In order that the plant may absorb the carbon dioxide so necessary to its growth, the leaves are furnished with tiny pores, called *stomata*, which are generally found only on the underside of the leaves and vary in number according to the type of the plant, but are on the average of from 100,000 to 1,000,000 per sq. inch of surface. Thus the economy of the plant calls for a set relation between the rate of absorption of the carbon dioxide, and the energy it uses to effect the combination into sugar.

If the rate of absorption of the gas is determined by the structure of the leaf—and in some plants the gas can diffuse easily, but in others with more difficulty—no increase in the amount of sunlight above that necessary to produce the appropriate amount of sugar from the absorbed gas can make the plant produce more. This is the basic scientific fact which determines that certain plants will grow better under conditions of shade or under conditions of more protracted sunlight, and for this reason it must be obvious to every gardener that a plant designed to grow in the shaded wood can seldom succeed when grown in conditions of full sunlight.

As the plant continues to grow it produces greater leaf surfaces and is continually in a position to use more of the energy derived from the sun until it ceases to produce more leafage and turns the products of its labours to flowers and to fruits; and here it seems certain that increased sunlight is necessary for the production of fruit and flowers. This is borne out by the fact that upon the production of the flower and seed of all monocarpic varieties the foliage diminishes and the plant perishes.

In the case of certain so-called hardy annuals the life-span of the plant can be prolonged for many years, exactly as in the case of the long-span monocarpic varieties, if the embryo flowers are persistently removed. Under these conditions a plant normally of only a few inches will often reach a height of several feet and continue to live for several years.

But to return to the question of the influence of the sunlight upon the growing green plant. We have stated that the production of the flowers and fruits calls for the increased use of sunlight. But it is not axiomatic that increased sunlight is followed by an increase in the quantity of either flower or fruit. The individual plant is extremely critical in its use of the light which falls upon it. If the length of day is increased by the use of artificial light, the plant should be able to continue to produce the sugar necessary for its sustenance and growth for a longer period. If, for example, melons or cucumbers are artificially lighted at night at an early age, they will flower earlier and grow quicker than plants not so lighted. But if they are grown in excessively bright sunlight the proportion of male flowers produced is increased, with a consequent falling off of the crop. In the case of chrysanthemums, however, a reduction of the amount of light which falls upon them will lead them to flower earlier than usual. Here the key to the situation is in the fact that the plants themselves normally flower because of certain conditions of natural lighting, that is, they flower at a period of the year when the day is "long", or when the day is "short", and if we induce these conditions artificially we can speed up the actual flowering. In the case, however, of some plants drawn from the tropics, where the length of day and night is approximately equal, an increase in the length of daylight seems to have the effect of delaying the flowering period, and a reduction in the amount of the daylight which falls upon them so that it does not greatly exceed twelve hours a day, will often succeed in making them flower not only earlier, but more profusely.

In the case of plants drawn from the higher latitudes it will be generally found that artificial illumination will induce earlier and better flowering. From this it will be seen to be of the first importance that the gardener should not only know the appropriate soil conditions for the growth of the plant, but also the periodicity of daylight under which it will best flourish.

It is not only the amount of light conveyed to the plant by the sun which affects its growth, however.

The temperature at which certain plants will flourish is extremely critical and varies in the case of many plants with the age, or stage of development, of the plant. Within limits, however the rate of chemical change within the plant itself rises as the temperature rises, and for each increase of $10°C$ may be said to be doubled. From this it would appear to be desirable that for the benefit of speedy growth the temperature should be as high as possible. There is, however, an optimum temperaure at which growth will no longer continue, and this temperature is variable in the case of different plants. This is equally true of insects and animals, and reminds one of the activity shown by certain of the caterpillars at varying temperatures, as exemplified by a story of three students. Discovering that a caterpillar will move more rapidly upon a sheet of warmed glass than upon a cold one, the first student proposed a contest to his friend. He promptly won by surreptitiously warming the sheet of glass in his hand. Having been told by his friend that the rising temperature led to greater chemical change, and consequently greater physical activity, the second student thought to profit by this learning to propose a similar contest to another friend. He thoroughly heated the glass before starting, only to lose the contest because, we are credibly informed, the caterpillar stopped periodically to blow upon each of its six feet in turn!

This increase in the speed of activity, as also applicable to plants, is amply illustrated by a correspondent from the Gold Coast. I had occasion some years ago to send out to a garden in that country some Aubrietas and a particularly virulent Loasa. The aubrietas, I was told upon enquiry, grew with great rapidity and were in a single season about two yards in diameter. They were in full flower in the morning, but without a single flower by noon. The Loasa, too, grew at a great rate, providing a most succulent meal for a giant native caterpillar, whose appetite was almost uniform with the rate of growth of the plant. I have always regretted that my correspondent returned home without being able to tell me which eventually proved victorious.

But to return to topics more serious. In the case of some tiny plants, such as the nitrogen-producing bacteria, the activity drops to nothing below 5°C, and reaches its maximum round about 28°C. This means that the maximum growth of many plants cannot be reached until this temperature is exceeded. As far as garden plants are concerned, the range of temperature at which they flourish is remarkable. Many alpine plants will grow perfectly well at a temperature only fractionally above freezing point, whereas the Dahlia gives its maximum growth somewhere between 14°C and 28°C. The maximum temperature at which most plants will grow appears to be in the neighbourhood of 50°C.

The influence of temperature upon the ripening of fruits is also critical. The presence or absence of sunlight, for instance, affects the ripening of tomatoes very little, but it is dependent upon a chemical change connected with the temperature. Thus

8. Prunus Cerasus var. Hisakura, a fine example of the flowering cherry

green tomatoes are best ripened by removing them from the plant and placing them in darkness, maintaining the temperature at between 60 - 70°F. The fungus Botyrites which sometimes affects these green fruits and causes them to spoil, grows badly in such a high temperature, particularly in a dry atmosphere, so that as a rule they remain unspoilt by such treatment.

# Chapter Nine

## OF DESIGN

"The Gryphon lifted up both its paws in surprise. "'What! never heard of uglifying,' it exclaimed. 'You know what to beautify is I suppose?' ' Yes,' said Alice doubtfully, 'It-means to-make-anything-prettier.'"

LEWIS CARROLL.

THE most important requirement of a garden is simplicity. The art of the garden-designer consists, wherever possible, in making one line do the work of two or many. This, however, does not imply that the art of garden-designing consists entirely in the use of either straight sweeps or single lines, for however straight the gardener may make his contours in the beginning, nature will take a hand to work them up into a variety of shapes. In the main, however, the lines of the garden are determined by the original design. I know of no method which can be used to greater effect by the man striving to build a garden upon a hitherto unused site, than to draw a scale plan of the plot and divide it to scale in the way in which he proposes to build his garden. He should set apart on the plan spaces to indicate the kitchen garden, the herbaceous borders, the shrubberies, the lawns, the paths—all the paraphernalia which go to make up the composite garden. In all probability much thought will be required suitably to site the paths and the concealing hedges, where these are required. With the aid of certain pieces of paper, also to scale, pieces of coloured loofah, and dabs of coloured plasticine it is possible for him to build up upon this original plan an adequate picture of the garden he has in his mind. He can determine in this manner, for instance, the height of the hedges required to screen the kitchen garden; to hide unwanted views from certain windows of the house; he may determine the character and size of certain shrubs needed to conceal until the last moment a particular view of

74

his garden which he may wish to reserve as a pleasant surprise for his casual visitors. He may judge, by cutting out small trees of loofah, the contours of shrubs best suited to certain sites; whether the tree required should be upright or weeping, standard or bush, whether it should have grey-green or golden-green foliage, and what the ultimate height should be to obtain the maximum effect. He may, if he so wishes, design and build a small rock garden, manufacturing his contours of plasticine, and his boulders of small pieces of gravel or stone. He can mend and alter to his heart's content, without bending his back or using more than one ounce of energy, knowing that he can see a result without having to wait for the passage of years.

The amateur garden-designer should remember that he has at least five points to bear in mind in addition to the first-mentioned lack of sophistication.

Firstly, I think, should come suitability, that is the ability of the design to knit in with the natural surroundings.

The second consideration I would describe by the word "pattern," by which I do not necessarily mean symmetry, but the general tendency of the garden to become a comprehensive whole in the sense that it is a complete entity without additions or excrescences.

Thirdly, I would stress the importance of contrast, by which again I do not mean that large and small trees should be grouped together indiscriminately, nor that flowers and shrubs of contrasting colours should be placed in immediate contact, but that the garden should contain within its borders beauty which is not only self-evident, but requires for its still greater glory the foil of some more sober neighbour. Nor must one omit the essential element of surprise. No garden should stand out to its creator on a single plane, and show one half of its splendours at a glance. It is better far that even its creator should be made to seek the beauty of his own handiwork in unsuspected places, as when rounding the corner of a sombre tree nothing could be more entrancing than to find jewels hidden in the grass. Used judiciously, the elements of surprise should be incorporated in even the smallest garden.

Finally, we come to perhaps the most vital element; constituent colour. No garden can ever satisfy one-tenth of man's normal aspirations unless it can show colour both in quantity, in variety, and in change. It is unsatisfactory from the angle of the bulk of all living things if they do not attain the object for which they were created. Thus a tree which fails to reach maturity is to be compared with a half-finished building; a flowering plant that refuses to flower, with a soured and embittered spinster. I have spent, in the course of half a lifetime, many pleasant hours wondering what the result would be when certain plants flowered which I had grown from seed sent to me by collectors, and I have had many pleasant surprises. But not one of them has ever reduced the insistent desire to survive long enough to see the remainder flower. But when perhaps once in the passage of ten years a single flower springs to life upon a hitherto unflowered plant, I feel that this is another beam of sunshine, in rather pleasant darkness. All is not sunshine however; I can well remember a group of seedlings reputed to be of a blue flower from Alaska, species unknown, which turned out to be a well-known British weed, with a small and insignificant yellow flower.

The employment of colour should take into account the varying tints of foliage, of flower, of fruit, and of surroundings. I have earlier suggested that the colour of an actual plant may be influenced to a very large extent in the eyes of the observer by its context, as it were, and the amateur designer should remember this; nor should he assume that his primary object is to dazzle the same observer's eye. Beauty can either flaunt herself, or creep into the overlooking eye and to the sympathetic heart in an almost imperceptible fashion. It all depends whether you prefer your charmer to be painted and sophisticated, or plain and ingenuous. Thus you create a garden to satisfy your own personal taste, not to obey a set of rules, or to please your neighbour. In this you may, in fact you should, please yourself.

The secret of a good garden is that it should be an almost complete expression of its owner's individuality, that it should not disclose all its secrets at once for the very same reason that if the owner's individuality is disclosed at one glance, he is most obviously a very shallow person; and finally that it should be different from all other gardens by reason of the fact that it was *not* better last week than it is this, and that it will not be better next week than it is now!

Assuming that the planning of the garden has been completed on paper as far as the layout of the main features is concerned, and their situation determined, the attention of the gardener may now be turned to the individual features. No garden can be regarded as complete without a well-kept grass lawn which will provide the solid mass of even green colouring which no other medium can supply, and which is the essential around which all colours may be brought into harmony. Undoubtedly the severity of the trimmed lawn is out of place in a wild garden and is best avoided in close proximity to the rock garden. It cannot be surpassed as a foil to the shrub garden, the borders, and the formal beds, for it is here that measured orderliness should prevail and the hand of man should provide cultural training, which adds sophistication to nature's prodigality.

A long-sighted gardener will take infinite care to ensure that the lawn shall be both pleasant and healthy. If he prefers a lawn which is flat and not crowned or undulating, he should see that the ground is levelled and well consolidated by rolling before the turf is laid or the seeds are sown. A good method by which this may be done is to tap in pegs with square tops which are allowed to project one inch above the surface of the ground immediately surrounding the peg. A straight-edge placed along the top of any two pegs and surmounted by a spirit level will immediately show in which direction the soil should be taken away. If one end of the straight-edge is continually moved to other pegs until the whole surface area has been covered, a very level piece of grass can be obtained.

Where it is impossible to secure a suitable native turf comparatively free of weeds, it is better to avoid turfing and use seed. Under these circumstances a good grass mixture, which excludes rye-grass, should be sown during September if possible, or failing this, as early in March as soil and weather conditions will allow. Pre-sown seed is probably the best medium for obtaining the required result.

A lawn should never be regarded as a means of placing a

large proportion of a garden under a crop which will make it trouble-free for ever, for it should be remembered that to retain its beauty and health it requires much attention, especially from the point of view of weeding and feeding.

Though approximately seven-eighths of the weight of grass cut each time the lawn is trimmed consists of water, one eighth consists of solid matter, some of which has been raised from the soil. Thus after a number of years of continuous cutting, the soil becomes impoverished especially in lime and phosphates. If this happens at a moderate rate, the coarse-leaved grasses are discouraged and are replaced by the finer-growing kinds, with a consequent improvement in the texture of the lawn, until the soil becomes acid or sour, as is shown by the development of bare patches which will not be fully covered again until the lawn has been treated with lime to remove the acidity, and phosphoric and potassic manures which will remedy the chemical deficiencies.

For a moment we will turn from lawns to hedges, where a variety of shrubs present themselves for mature consideration. In recent years *Cupressus macrocarpa* has been much used for hedges and tall screens, and wrongly so. It has the one great drawback of dying in patches when clipped, for no apparent reason, and presents the gardener with a difficult problem to solve when this takes place, as it does in an adult hedge. Nevertheless it is extremely effective upon chalky soils, and very good near the sea. On the whole, and for a similar purpose, either *Thuya plicata* or *Lobbii* is probably a better plant, and it grows just as quickly.

Two equally good Conifers are *Cupresses Lawsoniana* and *Thuya gigantea*, which are both imperturbable, and are best planted as small trees and clipped at the appropriate height.

Of all the shrubs which make good hedges the pride of place should I think be given to the genus Berberis. *Berberis stenophylla* makes a perfect evergreen hedge which can be clipped, and which bears masses of clusters of golden-yellow flowers in April and May, followed by blackish fruits. *Berberis Hookeri* is an equally good evergreen variety, with golden-orange flowers and purple-black fruits. *Berberis Wilsonae*, which often casts its leaves, which change colour in the autumn, has pale-gold flowers succeeded in the autumn with hanging clusters of salmon-red berries of exquisite beauty.

In town gardens, the ubiquitous privet hedge is only too often in evidence, but though it grows well, it seldom adds anything but dour rigidity to the garden. In a wild hedge, allowed to roam, its long spires of white scented flowers perfume the air delightfully, and are succeeded by sprays of luscious black berries.

For the town garden the close growth and bright green, small, neat leaves of *Lonicera nitida* are particularly apt, and if a few odd berries are produced in October, they are worth a moment's glance, for they are translucent pearls of purple-violet, which caught with the sun transmitted through them surpass even the beauty of rubies. *Lonicera yunnanensis* is larger in the leaf, somewhat quicker in growth, and larger in the berry, and also makes an excellent hedge.

It may be, however, that your taste for hedges entails a selection of colour as wide in range as that of Joseph's coat. A hedge to conjure memories, but which can be recommended to neither the faint-hearted nor the beginner, can be made of a variety of shrubs as wide in range as the components of a patch-work quilt. Alders, Berberis, Blackthorns, Lilacs, Lonicera, and Privet are mixed in confusion confounded. The lilacs are trained to top the hedge so that they are not clipped, the remainder indulge, with some restraining influence, in wild and bewildering entanglement. Some failures there will be, which after the dissipation of disappointment should be replaced with other shrubs, equally well chosen and trained to produce as thick and robust a growth as possible, and trained to become a coherent whole as soon as years and constant care can encourage. Such a mixed hedge will give more joy than one composed only of one kind of shrub; but it will also give more trouble. This is just as well, since the work of building such a hedge is primarily the work of the enthusiast.

An exceptionally good seaside hedge can be made of the Tamarix, but it is scarcely to be recommended elsewhere. The Common Beech, planted as a staggered hedge with intervals of two feet between the trees, can be kept closely clipped and form as solid a windbreak and as impenetrable a thicket as ever

Christian had to surmount, and in addition lend to the winter the comfort of its warm brown persistent leaves.

Many of the polyantha roses make the most delightful of hedges, and charm the summer to its inevitable end with colour, line and perfume. Such a one is *Donald Prior.* Nor must one forget the *Penzance Briars* which, if they suffer from a shortened flowering season, have the more evanescent charm of intangibility, persisting rather in the imagination than in reality.

After hedges what should follow but paths? And here a variety of choice exists such as to render the abundance an embarrassment of riches. Shall it be a grass path, one which will resemble a sward of deep green velvet? Perhaps winter will turn it into a Slough of Despond. Shall it be one constructed of crazy paving, for bad workmanship and consecutive frost to make it resemble a section of a bombed but tidied building? Shall it be gravel, which will gradually lose its erstwhile reddened smoothness and become patched with the evergrowing masses of encroaching moss?

Second thoughts suggest that broader treatment of the subject is as much to be desired as wider paths in the garden. Firstly consider whether the paths are to bear much traffic; whether they are to be used in periods of very wet or severe weather. Consider also if the soil is heavy or retentive of moisture. If all these things are so, let there be no grass path. Buried amidst a host of other memories is a recollection of such a path in which heavily laden barrows sank to the axles in wet weather. This was eventually remedied by sinking in the morass, masses of large clinker, then cordwood, clinker again, and so on until the fluid soil could only just reach the surface. Then, and only then, would the grass grow to remain. If, however, the soil is well drained and the traffic light, there can be no objection to the construction of grass paths, if they are kept wide so that the wear on the surface is not confined to a narrow band. In normal times I think a thin steel strip-edging, over which a roller can be taken when cutting has been done, obviates the trimming of the edges, and the constant setting-back, necessary to ensure complete tidiness.

Crazy paving can be both good or bad, but whether good or bad is seldom trouble-free unless it is set in cement with the joints hermetically sealed against the ingress of weed seeds. The stone for the surface should be selected with more than ordinary care. It should not flake; it should be of even colour and, at that, of a colour which blends with the surrounding features; it should also be slip-proof. Limestone slabs can be very treacherous in wet weather and should be used with the nicest care. It seems hard to believe that plants can grow in the very small pockets which should be left free of cement for this purpose, but they will, and do. Inefficiently laid crazy paving adds point to its name by its behaviour. Unless suitably bedded, like rumour, it rears an ugly head, and similarly spreads, unless the outermost bands of stones are firmly fixed so that such movement cannot take place.

I have no words to say in praise of cement paths except for the kitchen garden, where they have the double advantage of being easy to keep clean, and well able to resist even the roughest treatment. In the formal garden shaped stone paths, rectilinear or symmetrical, have their definite place, but paths of such design should be avoided in the neighbourhood of wild, natural, or rock gardens.

Gravel paths can be most attractive in some settings, and when well kept seem to add warmth to the surroundings. With paths, however, as with other things, satisfaction of personal taste is the object at which to aim, provided always that no natural solecism is thereby committed.

Having been led by various paths to the garden, we can break into a land where promise always overleaps performance, except on those rare occasions when one surpasses one's own expectations, and finds that what was expected to be a goose has really become a swan.

Let us look for a while at the sites we have fixed for the herbaceous borders. We have before us reasonably flat surfaces, well-dug and well-manured, stretching in two directions. We can use plants to provide us with the colours we desire, with sequences of variation in height, along the length of the bed. But obviously we must have the front of the border, if it faces only one way, and both the front and the back of the border, if it faces two ways, peopled with plants which diminish in height towards the edges of the bed. We must therefore plan our border in three dimensions, with little to guide us when we plant it—since the plants have then no tops—other than the knowledge we have already gained and held of the plants we wish to use, together with such information about our unknown quantities as may be obtained from catalogues, books and encyclopædias.

Obviously in a border which faces two ways we are likely to have, at least in summer, when growth is at its maximum, a side which is shaded at the base rather more densely than its somewhat sunnier neighbour. In our first selection of plants we should choose those which experience has shown delight in such conditions, to be placed on this side. We shall find that among these are numbered the Geums, the Phloxes, the Lupins, and the Asters. Since herbaceous borders are likely to be with us for ever, and memories are fleeting and gardeners far from omniscient, it is wise to make a plan showing the location of each group of plants as they are planted. During the first year of the existence of the border we note upon the plan all the plants which please us from the point of view of both colour, growth, and association, and things which displease us from the same points of view, so that we may duplicate such pleasant surprises as we may receive, and mend our own mistakes.

In the larger borders any adequate design must be based upon the masses of colour for effect, so that plants are grouped in numbers of from three to nine. Foliage plants, or plants with a long flowering period, should be chosen for the outer edges of the borders, where their height is suitable, or distributed in groups at intervals throughout the design. Plants which flower early should be placed in close company with those which flower later, so that no large colourless patches are seen for long periods.

Schemes specialising in the use of a short colour-range, that is, by using one colour only, are not difficult to make, but have one predominant disadvantage; they have also a short duration. Where several borders are incorporated in the design of the garden, this however should prove no deterrent, since one always finds another border which may be pleasing to the eye when others have long since passed that stage.

When taste dictates considerable range in a colour scheme,

care should be taken particularly that the so-called reds are not in offensive association, and the would-be designer should satisfy himself by experiment that he will not be overwhelmed by his own artistry. Seldom is the combination of orange, scarlet, and purple used satisfactorily, though this combination, with the added attraction and the silvery greys of the Artemisias, is one of the most striking features which can be incorporated in the border.

## Chapter Ten

### OF HERBACEOUS PLANTS

"Alice was not surprised at this, she was getting so used to
queer things happening, while she was looking at the place
where it had been, it suddenly appeared again."

LEWIS CARROLL.

IN the herbaceous border what shall we grow? We have previously stated that our selection of plants for any garden will
be dictated by the character of the soil and the aspect in which
the plants are to grow. The final criterion should be one of fit-
ness. Some time ago a correspondent sent me a very fine picture
of a very fine rock garden designed by a very fine artist. The
photograph was an expensive coloured production by an excellent
photographer. The design was simple and pleasing. But the
owner had "improved" it by planting masses of geraniums to
add colour. My own comment was confined to appreciation of
the design of the garden, and I added, if I remember aright,
that the geraniums were good specimens of their kind. In point
of fact pelargoniums and rock gardens have no affinity. Each
is at home and in character only when judged by its surroundings. It is no far cry from Geraniums to pixies, gnomes, and
elves tripping, if indeed they could dance, around fantastic toad-
stools of scarlet spotted with gold—or to conclude upon a note
of banality—cement frogs, lizards, or rabbits.

Where should we draw a line between plants which are, or
are not, suitable for the herbaceous border? Here I must confess
I number myself among the Philistines, and often include in
the bed plants which are annual, plants which are bulbous, and
plants which are normally used for bedding purposes. Since
the border has largely become the home for a great number of
florists' varieties, there can be no substantial objection to this.
I see no reason, however, why shrubs and plants of persistent
woody growth should find a place here, unless their habit of

9. Rhododendron Wardii, a Chinese Rhododendron of the "Souliei" group

growth allows them to be treated in precisely the same way as herbaceous plants. Among those which deserve special mention are the following, all of which are worth a place in the border if not in the sun.

Earlier we have discussed the question of names. The plants I shall select will therefore bear their catalogued specific and varietal names. Once you have acquired them you may speedily forget them if you wish. One of the most fascinating gardens I ever visited was that in which every plant was known by the name of its donor. Thus a group of Mallows was known as Colonel Blimp, a fine Aster as Mrs. Brown, a patch of Gentians as Commander Campbell, and a Moon-daisy as Miss Pigott, and so on. This may be a precedent to follow if your friends alone furnish your garden, but if ever it becomes necessary to buy a plant yourself you may find that what the catalogue calls CHRYSANTHEMUM MAXIMUM is merely another alias for poor Miss Pigott.

*Antholyza* is a bulbous plant reminiscent of the Gladiolus, which adapts itself so kindly to the garden that it forms stout but graceful turves of sword-shaped leaves, from which upon a day in late summer its friendly red and gold flowers rise in spires to delight the eye. It can be left in the ground throughout the winter, and when at last it is uprooted for division its accumulated corms stand one upon the other like a string of underground beads.

*Aquilegia longissima* is a very long-spurred columbine from America with spurs which stand out like Mr. Mantovani's whiskers, or extend in the graceful curves of a colourful but gentle octopus. *Aquilegia longissima* grows equally well in the sun or shade in good, fertile soil, and is best produced from the seed which it freely forms.

Of all the Delphiniums the later introductions are undoubtedly the most prepossessing. *Delphinium macrocentron*, which comes from Kenya, is short, stout, and has but few flowers on a stem. The spur stands straight up, so that each flower looks like a ballet dancer with a wind-swept skirt. But the colour is the thing, for here, when a good form is obtained, the flower is of sombre, dull green, surprisingly lit here and there with flashes of brilliant emerald, and over-laid inside the flower with azure-blue. Nor must one forget *Delphinium Welbyii*, probably the most outstanding of all. It grows to about three feet in height, has very few, very large flowers, very widely and openly dispersed on long, loose stems and of an attractive shade of Cambridge-blue. Endemic to Abyssinia, is has so far proved perfectly hardy in this country.

Another friendly plant is *Diascia*. Listed in most seedsmen's catalogues as an annual, it is a good perennial, more especially in its Gibraltar form, which is of a soft salmon-pink. It forms a mass of stems which continuously bear double-spurred flowers in short spires.

*Gypsophila repens* is a well-known plant used in the larger rock gardens. It now has a relative in *Gypsophila repens rosea flore pleno*, which has double pink flowers, borne in tumbling masses which make it resemble an effervescing froth. It has but one fault, the stems where they join the tap root are but gently anchored, and a high wind will bear them away when the large floral heads act as a sail; it should therefore be planted in some shelter.

*Hedysarum coronarium* is a plant which produces upon its green sappy stems with light-green foliage, small spikes of crimson pea-flowers for a long period, and though that curious plant *Incarvillea grandiflora* with its queer, horse-radish-like roots bears its few flowers only for a few days at most, and its colour is a quaint purplish-pink, its huge size and its wide, frank face make it an extraordinarily attractive plant.

A splendid plant for any shady place is *Kirengeshoma palmata*, which is normally at home in Japan, with its pale-green, fig-like leaves and dainty, pale-yellow, five-petalled flowers hanging from green calices. Its propensity to provide this beauty in September commends it greatly.

The *Kniphofias*, or red-hot poker plants which are also known as Tritomas, have a peculiarly rigid beauty with *Kniphofia Nelsonii* the least stiff and the smallest of the species.

No gardener can afford to be without specimens of the *Linums* or flax plants. *Linum narbonense* bears deep-blue, open flowers in sprays on thin but wiry stems which rise to about three feet in height in such prodigality, and with such grace, that it must be worth the few pence which will acquire it honestly; *Linum viscosum* is stouter in the stem and has larger leaves, which are sticky to the touch. It bears large flowers of lavender-pink, deepening to blue in the centre.

Of the lilies I incline to *Lilium monadelphum*, var. *Szyovitizianum*, which stands in rigid splendour on a stout but daintily planned stem of about four feet in height, and bears flowers with six curved petals of pale golden-yellow which are slightly flashed with purple at the base and side. The flowers of *Lilium Dalhansonii*, which John Hinde has caught so well in Plate VI are smaller, but there are many more of them. The buds are not so graceful, but they have a more symmetrical distribution, are of deep red-brown, quaintly flecked here and there with orange, and bear all the polish of old and well-cared-for mahogany. The genus LOASA, sometimes called BLUMENBACHIA, is related to the stinging nettle, and some of its members bite much more virulently. A curious plant, and one which was once used as a mild corrective for the more exuberant members of our junior staff, since we found that it propagated most easily from stem cuttings. The punishment was eventually dropped because it was found that the only person the plant did not sting was the one most often detailed to deal with it. The flowers of at least two varieties are bright orange and very large with five incurling petals.

In passing to the Lupin, one cannot help but be struck with the development of plants which have lost the basic colouring of the original wildlings. For instance *Delphinium Ruysii* has a very fine pink colour and can be one of the most attractive of all plants if one can accommodate one's mind to accepting a Delphinium which is any colour but blue. This criticism, however, could hardly be allowed against the Lupin, into which every colour of the rainbow now seems to have crept, vying with the spectrum in passing through white, yellow, orange, crimson, violet, maroon, and blue. But here I think that the most attractive plan is to confine Lupins to a border for themselves,—not to grow them with the idea of producing a shaded range of colour-variation, but rather in the same way as that confectioner of my early years made his hundreds and thousands in belts and bands and mixtures, with no regard for set orderliness.

The genus MECONOPSIS is represented in the minds of most people by *Meconopsis Baileyii* or, more correctly, *Meconopsis betonicaefolia*, the blue Himalayan poppy, which is undeniably beautiful when grown in a soil free of lime, when it retains its blue and gold colouring unsoiled by purple. In a calcareous soil the colour is degraded to such an extent that it becomes quite unattractive. *Menocopsis Baileyii* is described with almost arithmetical impartiality as biennial, monocarpic, and perennial, with extraordinary charm of both truth and candour. In fact it may be any of these things, according to the way in which it is grown. Quite frequently the plant flowers before it has produced offsets, and then dies after fruiting; if, however, offsets are encouraged before it flowers (this can be done by pinching out the flowering tips) it can be induced to become perennial, and will wax wider and more lush, and will live to delight the eye with floods rather than flashes of colour (Plate VII). It is best grown in a leafy soil in a position where it is lit only by filtered sunlight. *Meconopsis regia* makes an enormous ring of pale green leaves covered with dense silvery hair, the rosettes being sometimes as much as five feet in diameter. The flowering spire is about six feet in height. It is conical in form and carries branching sprays of very large yellow flowers. At its best it does not flower until it is five or six years of age, and dies after flowering. *Meconopsis grandis* has the bluest flowers of all when a plant of good parentage is obtained; its large, deep blue flowers being raised to a height of nearly three feet on stout but graceful stems, *Meconopsis grandis* is one of the true perennial Meconopses and thrives under similar conditions to those which suit *Meconopsis Baileyii*. My own special favourite is the monocarpic variety *Meconopsis Dwhojii* from Nepal, which makes a ring of pale blue-grey feathery foliage, densely overlaid with extremely long, bronze-gold hair. After a heavy dew and with the sunlight just touching it, it is the outstanding beauty. By some people the flowering spike is held to be disappointing, but its pale yellow flowers fit its attractive rosette so well that to change colour or shape could not improve it. The last Meconopsis to mention is *Meconopsis quintuplinervia*, another perennial which quickly forms a mat of short, broad leaves. The flowers are of lavender-blue, deepening to purple at the centre, pendent in the manner of the harebell, but seeming almost too large for the frail stem to lend them support.

It does not need a great deal of imagination to endow the plants in the garden with personalities, and to regard them as little people with charms or idiosyncrasies, and wills of their own. *Melittis melissophyllum* (the honey-balm) becomes personified as the clown in the circus. It forms a rotund shrubby growth of rough green leaves, and produces from the leaf-axils musk-like flowers of white, with large, symmetrical flashes of orchid-purple on nose and cheeks. In addition the foliage is ineffably scented. One of the most delightful of all garden plants, it is easy to grow, but is seldom found in a garden.

Another plant with a personality is *Mertensia virginiana*. This has attractive pale glaucous foliage of pleasing shape, and grows to a height of two feet; it produces open, fairy-like sprays of pink buds, which open to flowers of clear pale blue. Many sprays are borne by one plant at the same time, so that a good plant appears to have as many flowers as there are stars in the Milky Way. *Mertensia virginiana* should be grown in leafy soil on the shady side of the border, when it will delight all observers in the early year.

It is not always the appearance of a plant which gives rise in one's mind to a particular association. The genus OENOTHERA compels the association in my own mind which makes me call it the wine-bibber. It was supposed in earlier times that the root of *Oenothera biennis*, when properly treated and administered, encouraged a taste for wine in the recipient. It seems strange that such a characteristic should be deemed worthy of notice, and it forces to my mind a further association with the advertisement that we used to see many years ago, headed " Smoking cured in three days." However, in this particular genus there are many beauties. The botanist has, however, had a great deal of fun; he has divided those plants, which once upon a time we knew as OENOTHERA, into a large number of genuses with different names. Some which come to mind are Megapterium, Michauxia, Kneiffia, Hartmannia, and Taraxia. But for garden purposes we shall retain the old name of OENOTHERA. Of them all *Oenothera glauca Fraserii* is probably the most attractive as its red stems and buds form such a delightful contrast to the large flowers of gleaming gold.

The genus OXALIS provides among its various species many extremely attractive plants. One cannot forget the astonishing generosity of *Oxalis floribunda* if one has ever seen it in full flower from early summer until the first frost compels it to seek winter refuge. Those of you who have ponds and keep fish should make sure not to plant a member of this genus near the banks, since it seems to exercise an attraction to various kinds of fish —with fatal results. *Physostegia virginiana* is a very exceptional occupant for the border for it flowers in September, and with my dog SCAMP provides the two most obedient occasional visitors. The flowers are bright pink, shaped like snapdragons with thin noses, but joy of joys, each seems to be joined to the stem with a ball and claw joint, and when moved to or fro will stay just where it is put. Such obedience is commendable both in dog and plant. Would that *Convolvulus* would so behave!

Nor should the border be without *Platycodon grandiflorus*, which is sometimes called the Chinese balloon-flower. I first made my acquaintance with this plant in Farringdon Street market, over thirty years ago. A hawker, who was apparently not making a fortune at his work, was selling tiny packages which contained, so he said, the Chinese balloon-flower and the flame-vine. Sixpence was the price demanded, and upon satisfaction of the demand one was able to examine the contents of the envelope, which proved to be one piece of stalk, resembling a piece of couch-grass, and a dried-up tuber, looking like a very small, old, wrinkled parsnip. These were duly planted and cared for. The parsnip-like growth eventually developed into a plant of about eighteen inches in height and bore from August onwards large balloon-shaped buds of smoky blue, which opened into Campanula-like flowers of soft blue, veined with purple. It is so hardy that all the plants I have now are descended from the original parsnip! The dried-up stem turned out to be *Tropaeolum speciosum*, and it was not quite so accommodating as the *Platycodon*, for it failed to put in an appearance either then or later, and I would urge all who wish to grow it well, to start with established plants rather than the bare root which resembles the common Bindweed.

The POLYGONUMS which are the knotweeds have the reputation of being roistering and rowdy occupants of the herbaceous border, behaving with the boisterousness of the boy in his teens. *Polygonum Bistorta* adds to this the charm of deep-green, heavily netted foliage on smooth red stems, with sprays of flowers of soft shell-pink, which has all the charm and modesty of the lily-of-the-valley. This colour is repeated in the bottle-brush, *Poterium obtusum*, the flower of which looks like a fairy-like edition of its namesake, but for real modesty a rather less sophisticated sister in *Poterium obtusum album* wins my greatest affection. So rarely does the white flower have a greater appeal that this is worth noting.

A plant seldom seen in the border is *Salvia uliginosa*, which forms an upstanding bush with straight stems and a few narrow leaves, crowned with rather narrow spires of dainty pale blue flowers, rather small individually but impressive in bulk. This is equally true of *Thalictrum dipterocarpum*, which has foliage like the Maidenhair Fern, very open and diffuse sprays of small flowers, borne on very thin stems. The outer petals always are of deep lavender, and the stems of gold and cream. Established in rather a moist spot in the border, it survives from year to year, increasing in charm. The double-flowered form is a really good plant and should certainly be grown in every garden.

I find on looking back that a large number of the herbaceous plants selected for special mention are varieties which flower late in the year, when the normal border is becoming dull, but this I feel needs no apology. To those already mentioned I will add *Stokesia cyanea* which appears in flower in September like a large lavender-blue Sweet Sultan, and is then even more welcome than its early simulacrum.

For the back of the border nothing can be better than *Verbena bonariensis*, whose thin but tough stems stand literally four-square and branch to produce similar stems, each bearing a rather small head of attractive, deep mauve flowers. It should be pointed out that this is impressive only when planted in bulk. This criticism cannot be levelled at *Verbena corymbosa*, which grows to about four feet in height and bears many heads of sweetly scented heliotrope flowers, reminiscent in every way of the plant of that name. Hardy beyond all doubt, it continues to increase in growth and appeal from season to season.

*Zauschneria mexicana*, or the Californian Fuchsia as it is some-times called, is one of the few shrubs which is at home in the herbaceous border, since the whole of its overground growth is killed in the winter. Growing to about one foot in height, and flowering from September until frozen into inactivity, it is admirably suited to the front of the border, where it will quickly take possession and produce its brilliant orange-scarlet flowers with great freedom, provided always that it is given a sufficiently hot and dry situation.

The plants discussed so far for the herbaceous border are not intended to be representative, nor are they in any way a complete selection. They are intended merely as a guide, to show some of the more valuable plants which seldom find their homes in the right places.

10. The seed heads of Clematis macropetala

## Chapter Eleven

## OF SHRUBS FOR THE WALL AND GARDEN

" 'Come, there's half my plan done now! How puzzling all these changes are! I'm never sure what I'm going to be from one minute to another! However, I'm back to my right size; the next thing is, to get into that beautiful garden, how is that to be done, I wonder?' As she said this she suddenly came upon an open place, with a little house in it. . . ."

LEWIS CARROLL.

NOW we come to a short discussion of how to plan a shrub garden. Here the early device of using pieces of loofah and paper to show the varying heights and scopes of the plants is to be recommended in planning. It is probably easier to design a shrub garden than a herbaceous one, mainly because the persistent tops of the shrubs remain in evidence when they are planted, and because the pattern reveals itself immediately upon planting. One additional factor however must be borne in mind, namely that the foliage colours of shrubs play a much more important part than those of herbaceous plants, since by habit of growth, their foliage colours are brought more closely to the eye. There are many books in existence which give the height to which certain shrubs will attain; there are few which denote the scope or the spread to which such shrubs will grow. It is disappointing after having waited several years for a shrub garden to develop, to find that a number of shrubs have to be removed because they are too closely planted. On the other hand, in the case of nearly all shrubs other than Conifers, efficient and systematic pruning can keep them to the desired shape and help them to fit more appropriately into the pattern as a whole. Select your shrubs from three points of view: 1. The shape, which includes also height; 2. The foliage, having regard to its persistence or otherwise and its normal colour; 3. The flowers, taking into consideration the colour and the period of the year in which the shrub normally flowers.

In the main, the small shrub garden should be built about certain outstanding features which should in general be the larger trees, such as the flowering cherries, crabs or almonds. (Plate VIII). The names of the flowering cherries are unfortunately much confused. *Prunus fugensis* (J. H. Veitch), *Prunus sakiyuma*, (Hisakura), or *Prunus Okumiyako* are among the best. Among the crab-apples *Malus John Downey*, *Malus Eleyii*, *Malus floribunda* variety *atro-sanguinea*, or *Malus purpurea* are of great worth, as indeed is *Malus aldenhamensis*, and all can be relied upon to charm the eye of the discerning; to quicken the heart-beat of the most sluggish, and to implant in the mind of the thoughtful an impression which will be left when petals have fallen and leaves have withered.

One of the finest of all trees for the garden is the flowering peach, *Prunus persicus;* above all I like the one which is called Clara Meyer, the full double flowers of which seem to hover on the margin of Phlox-pink and Neyron-rose, and one must not forget the common almond, *Prunus communis* or, as it was once known, *Amygdalus communis*, a harbinger of Spring too well-known to need description, but far too attractive to be vaguely dismissed.

I have made no mention of the overriding decisive facts: the aspect of the site and the character of the soil, since earlier I have stressed the importance of the soil and the incidence of sunshine.

In no shrub border can one omit the Maples. *Acer Negundo variegatum* with its green stems, bright green and cream variegated foliage, is always outstanding in the background. *Acer japonicum* and *Acer palmatum* both have ornamental foliage, which in the dissectum group is of fine, much-cut outline and of the lightness of fairyland and varies in colour from bright green to the deep blood-red of *Acer purpureum*. The septemlobum group have foliage almost as finely cut as that of the dissectum group, in fact in some cases even more so, and has the same range of entrancing colours.

Normally the Maples of this type are grafted on to stocks of a quicker-growing variety, and lose their character as a result very rapidly. They are not, however, impossible to obtain upon their own roots. Where it is desired that they should remain slow-growing and dwarf, it is wise to make sure that they are thus grown.

A rather attractive plant for the front of the shrub garden is *Aplopappus ericoides*, which has grey-green leaves like heather, and bears sprays of deep yellow daisy flowers; it reaches three feet in height, is perfectly hardy, and like the old lady, who knits well, talks well, and smiles often, is a very nice person to know.

The use of ARTEMISIAS with their attractive aromatic foliage-variations is certainly to be encouraged in the front of the garden. The best known of these is the Southernwood or Old Man. In such an appealing family it is perhaps as well that the most senile should be least attractive, for the Old Man's younger brothers, sons, and daughters have charms which attract followers as hounds follow the scent.

Another remarkable plant is *Abutilon megapotamicum*, or *vexillarium*, which rarely exceeds five feet in height and a little less in diameter, and combines quaintly-shaped excentrically centred green leaves with hanging balloon-shaped buds, reminiscent of the Cape Gooseberry, *Physalis Franchettii*. The buds first of all are pale green, but deepen to vinous red and open to let fall a skirt of Chinese yellow, from which stands out a large cluster of maroon stamens for all the world like a miming Columbine. The great advantage to be derived from this Abutilon is its extremely long period of flowering, for it begins to flower in June and continues until the end of the year. A sheltered position and a soil with little lime, suffice to keep it happy, but in the more inclement North it should be situated against the South wall, where it will prove an admirable plant, admired alike by its possessor and his friends who, coveting its beauty, will beg both its name and its cuttings.

Of all the plants of which the garden deserves well, one cannot speak more highly than of the BERBERIS, of which *Berberis rubrostilla*, *Berberis stenophylla*, *Berberis Thunbergii* and its variety *atro-purpurea* should on no account be omitted, but the superlatives must be reserved for *Berberis lologensis*, whose red-orange buds, and orange flowers merit the richness of the royal purple.

Without a doubt the finest sight I have seen this year has been a hedge of *Berberis subcauliata* which, though deciduous, was so heavily clothed with berries in the late autumn as to compel attention rather than request it. All the Barberries provide fruit which makes jelly of a flavour to tempt the palate of Lucullus, but beware of employing them to make jam, for the seeds are as innumerable as diatoms in the sea.

*Buddleia*, especially those of the *Davidii* type, produce under some circumstances so many seedlings as to be nearly as difficult to eradicate as the most persistent of weeds. Most of the species are exceptionally floriferous and prove as attractive to the gardener as to the butterflies, which on a sunny day cover the long spires of deep lavender flowers, borne on bushes often exceeding ten feet. Unfortunately the racemes are persistent after they die, when, like corpses, they are by no means prepossessing. *Berberis alternifolia*, with its smaller, darker foliage and smaller, scented flowers of creamy lilac, is a more fascinating plant, but was one of the casualties in the severe winter of 1940. *Berberis globosa*, on the other hand, with its small, round, honey-scented orange clusters, is hardy and indefatigable, and though its period of flowering is not long, it is worth a place in the sun at the back of the garden, where it reaches ten feet in height.

Among the autumn-flowering plants which must be included in the shrub garden is that delightful Caryopteris, *Caryopteris clandonensis*, which produces large clusters of much frilled, lavender-blue flowers late in the year, and together with the deep blue plumbago-like flowers of *Ceratostigma Wilmottianum* helps to hasten the year to its end with flowers so completely unsuited to mourning, that one imagines the year piped away by cloven-footed Pan.

We ought not to omit mention of *Ceanothus*, of which the varieties *dentatus*, *rigidus*, *Veitchianus* and *Burkwoodii* are more or less evergreen, with Burkwoodii flowering probably longer than any of the other. In addition, *Ceanothus Gloire de Versailles* has larger flowers and lives for a longer flowering period, but is apt to drop its leaves in winter. It has pale lavender-blue flowers, and has a hybrid relation called Albert Pittet, with flowers of pale rose. Many of the varieties, especially the first four, can be kept to shape by heavy pruning, which should be

11.  Phlox subulata Camlaensis, a rock garden Maid-of-all-work

done immediately on the conclusion of flowering; but to retain the vigour and active character of a plant under these circumstances, feeding should take place in the second year.

All these varieties other than *Ceanothus Gloire de Versailles* and *Albert Pittet* flower on the previous year's wood, and should be pruned immediately after flowering. *Gloire de Versailles* and *Albert Pittet* flower on the current year's wood and should therefore be pruned in March, or even earlier.

*Chimonanthus fragrans*, or the winter-sweet, produces its flowers during the winter; they are a very pale straw-yellow centred with ruby-maroon, and the scent is that of the Narcissus. It is not essential to grow it near a wall, though usually it is grown near the windows of the house for the benefit of its undeniable fragrance. It should be encouraged by heavy pruning, immediately after flowering, to produce the new young wood upon which it will so readily flower the next season, for to spare the knife will but spoil it for a season.

Another shrub usually placed near a window for the benefit of its almond-scented flowers is *Choisya ternata*, the Mexican Orange-blossom, which makes a large bush with bright green highly polished leaves, clusters of clear white flowers resembling orange-blossom produced in early spring, and as if to speed the parting year, again in the autumn. It is cut by frost during severe winters, but this appears merely to encourage it to grow still further, though, sad to relate, it often prevents it from producing its so sweetly-scented flowers.

The *Cydonias*, or Japanese Quinces have in addition to a variety of names a great range of colour. The plain Japonica of gardens is really *Cydonia lagenaria*. The flowers in shape and production are reminiscent of large apple-blossoms, glamorised with heavily pollened stamens and highly painted petals. The gamut of colour is great, ranging from the deepest dark red to pure white.

*Cydonia Japonica*, that is the *Cydonia Mauleii* of gardens grows only to four feet, compared to double this height in the case of *Cydonia lagenaria*; the colour range is nearly as great. There are a number of hybrids, the two species which also provide shrubs of similar characteristics. Both types bear large, late fruits from which a jelly can be made which is edible except to the epicure. Flowering mainly in the spring, *Cydonia lagenaria* begins to flower in February, and *Cydonia Japonica* in April. Both are of easy culture, and though they are usually found sited against a south wall, grow with freedom and complete hardiness almost anywhere, as if to confirm that:

"Full many a flower is born to blush unseen,
  And waste its sweetness upon the desert air."

There is probably no shrub with a greater measure of popularity than the broom, *Cytisus scoparius*, from which sprang the variety *Cytisus Andreanus*, with its bright yellow pea-flowers with centres of red-brown. This has given rise to the many-coloured modern varieties with crimson and gold flowers, of which Dorothy Walpole is one of the best crimsons, Firefly, of the two-coloured shades, and Cornish Cream, a delightful cream-coloured species with a colour reminiscent of moonbeams, soft music, and running water. Unfortunately brooms dislike transplanting and fail if left out of the ground too long. It is a wise precaution for the would-be grower to insist that they should have been pot-grown, and during their first year of establishment he should adequately water and care for them. Other species worthy of special note are the prostrate *Cytisus Kewensis*, with cream-coloured flowers, and *Cytisus praecox*, of similar colour; *Cytisus albus* with white pea-flowers on slender wands, and *Cytisus purpureus* with rose-pink flowers freely produced on arching stems.

No shrub garden can afford to omit some representatives of the Cistus family. A personal favourite is *Cistus Skanbergii*. It comes from the island of Lampedusa and forms a very compact shrub of neat growth with glaucous grey foliage, and produces clustered heads of buds, opening to pink buttercups, of a tint defying description. This, in spite of its place of origin, is one of the hardiest. Other delightful varieties are *Cistus Silver Pink*, the name of which describes its colour, for its soft pink flowers seem overlaid with silver; *Cistus purpureus*, with very large pink flowers showing a characteristic patch of maroon at the base of the petal, and *Cistus ladaniferus* and *laurifolius*, both with large white flowers. Two of the family which are quite different in habit are *Cistus rosmarinifolius*, which has leaves like those of the Rosemary, and small white flowers like open white buttercups, a somewhat similar plant is *Helianthemum libanotis*, which has flowers of the same shape but which gleam with borrowed gold.

A plant for which I hold a large measure of affection is *Crinodendron Hookerii*, or as it is often known, *Tricuspidaria Hookerii*, which thrives best in a shady site in a lime-free soil. The attractive dark-green evergreen foliage forms an enchanting foil for the bright crimson flowers which hang upon long stems like miniature Chinese lanterns. Placed in such a position as is detailed the plant appears to be perfectly hardy, grows to about five feet in height, and exerts a charm which will open the purse of even the most miserly to produce the five shillings which will make it his own.

Of DAPHNES I have no words but words of praise; each member of the genus confers grace upon the garden. *Daphne Blagayana* forms a low, spreading bush which roots, in suitable soil, where it touches the ground, and produces in March and April large clusters of somewhat small, clear creamy-white flowers, the scent of which is so pronounced as to lead one to expect an exotic and to seek to find its source wherever it may be. Farrer calls attention to its needs when he says " Each passer-by should cast a limestone boulder as he passes," since if the stem of this particular variety is covered with loose stones in the form of a cairn it will soon become honeycombed with vigorous flowering stems. *Daphne Cneorum*, or the Garland Flower, grows to about one foot in height and fares best if it is covered each year to about half of its height with a fresh mixture of peat-mould and limestone chippings. One spray of *Daphne Cneorum* or *Daphne Blagayana* will scent a whole room. *Daphne collina*, which grows to two feet, has substantial heads of lilac-pink which at times appears dingy, but at others as entrancing as any other charmer, and the characteristic scent of the genus, though its leaves are wider and more grey than any other. An interesting hybrid known as *Daphne Somerset*, which is of the parentage of *Daphne Cneorum* and *Daphne caucasica*, is probably the easiest of all to grow. It grows to about three feet in height and produces many small clusters of pale pink flowers, paling to white, and carried the characteristic scent. *Daphne mezereum* is deciduous, flowering before the leaves are borne, generally in January or February. It can be obtained in varieties with flowers which are either purplish-pink or white, and forms a leafy bush up to four feet in height. The exquisitely scented clustered flowers are followed by acrid and poisonous berries. The white variety *Daphne mezereum alba* is exceptionally attractive; the berries which follow are yellow.

*Daphne rupestris* is the most charming dwarf, seldom exceeding six inches in height, with larger flowers than most of the species, and similar fragrance. It is most frequently found grafted upon a stock of *Daphnelaureola* or *Daphne Mezereum*, and as a result is out of character. Such a procedure gives rise to no advantage but speed in growth, and as *Daphne rupestris* is easy to grow upon its own stem the discerning gardener will insist that it should be so grown. This is a plant to nurse and to nourish, to caress and to care for; for of the whole galaxy this is the star of stars.

*Daphne retusa* is another dwarf of twelve to eighteen inches, with a stout stem, reminiscent of a miniature laurel stem, somewhat fleshy in character and clad with narrow polished dark green leaves, and bearing purple buds which open white. The scent is both searching and unforgettable, permeating the senses to such a degree as for ever to remain a fragrant memory.

The ERICAS or Heaths have their place in shrub plantings either for the brightness which they bring early in the year, or for the ground cover they afford for the deciduous Rhododendrons. The winter-flowering types are mainly indifferent to lime and bring colour when it is hardest to obtain; plantings of *Erica carnea* and its varieties: *King George*, *Mrs. S. Doncaster*, *Vivelli*, *Springwood White* and *Springwood Pink*, are all to be desired. *Erica carnea*, variety *Vivelli*, puts all others in the shade, for its depth of colour makes all the others seem but pale shadows. *Erica praecox rubra* is also an outstandingly good variety of bright colour and can be followed by the more upstanding *Erica mediterranea hybrida* and *Erica stricta*. These *Ericas* benefit from clipping back after flowering to a point just below that at which they flowered.

The Cornish and Connemara Heaths, *Erica vagans*, *Daboecia cantabrica* and their varieties are calcifuge and should be planted only in lime-free soils in conjunction with other lime-haters like the Azaleas and Rhododendrons. The best Cornish Heaths are undoubtedly *Erica vagans*, Mrs. *Maxwell* and *Erica vagans*, St. *Keverne*, both of which avoid any blue-blooded taints, at least in colour. The Irish Heath has larger leaves and flowers and varies from deep-purple to white in colour in its varieties.

Forsythia heralds the spring with a foretaste of golden sunshine, lavish as a spendthrift's dream. The gaiety of the long strands of hanging "golden-bells" ensure it a place in every shrub border, *Forsythia suspensa* is the most widely grown variety and its drooping branches add to its charm. Even better is the ten foot *Forsythia intermedia*, a hybrid with larger flowers and freer flowering, if that be possible. *Forsythia intermedia* variety *primulina*, has paler flowers, and variety *spectabilis* larger flowers than the type. *Forsythia Giraldii* is earlier than any, and more graceful than most. Forsythias should be pruned where necessary immediately after flowering, as they flower on the previous year's wood. *Corylopsis pauciflora*, which resembles a dwarf and pale refined version of the Forsythia, is nearly as lovely, the pale green bracts which envelop the flowers shading the wintry cream of the petals with complete artistry. *Corylopsis Gotoana* is later, has smaller flowers, but has the charm of even more artistic distribution.

The Fuchsia can be a good plant for the sheltered shrub garden, though it is liable to be cut by frosts in certain winters. The best type for the purpose is *Fuchsia macrostemma* with its red and purple flowers, and *Fuchsia macrostemma alba*, with pale pink petals and pale lavender corolla. Both grow to at least six feet in height. The high spot of the genus is the tender *Fuchsia fulgens* with its long, tubed, slender flowers of bright scarlet with green tips. In a sheltered garden, placed against a south wall, it will prove a source of pleasure all summer.

Such a pleasant name is that of the Witch Hazel, divorced from the unguent to which the plant has given its name. This is derived from *Hamamelis virginiana*, which produces its pleasant and fragrant flowers in the autumn, and is outshone and outscented by the Chinese Witch Hazel, *Hamamelis mollis*, which produces its flowers in the winter on its bare stems. Tiny ragged

tongues of gold extrude from the central zones of deep red, and if the gardener is urged to cut the twigs for the benefit of its fragrant flowers, provided this is done with decorum and sympathy, both the shrub and he will profit much thereby. This messenger will bear its good tidings whatever its native soil may be.

Another shrub bearing a name with which to conjure is *Hibiscus syriacus*, which forms a shapely bush, reaching as much as six feet in height, and bearing in conjunction with its pale green leaves flowers like those of the hollyhock, in white, pink, and lavender-blue; there is also a double-flowered variety. Succeeding well upon any soil, it deserves a sheltered and warm corner of the border. It flowers well upon the new wood and may be pruned severely in the autumn or spring without disadvantage.

The HYDRANGEA has unfortunate associations with the Aspidistra, but has one relative at least, *Hydrangea Sargentiana*, which forms a great, upstanding bush of up to twelve feet with large green woolly leaves about a foot long, and bears panicles of white sterile flowers centred by rose-purple florets, insignificant in themselves, but impressive in the mass. Grown in a somewhat shaded spot, it is one of the most outstanding of plants.

Of HYPERICUMS there is no end; this is fortunate, since there is also no end to their flowering capacity and their extreme usefulness. For clothing a rough bank, nothing could be more opportune and invasive than *Hypericum Calycinum*, but the real beauty of the genus is more clearly typified in *Hypericum Moserianum* which is a low-growing shrub with very large golden-yellow flowers with a central cluster of thread-like stamens. *Hypericum Moserianum tricolor*, has leaves edged with red and white, and red-bronze buds. *Hypericum patulum*, variety *Henryii* is more vigorous and equally beautiful, and *Hypericum patulum* (variety *Forrestii*) has arching sprays and a long flowering period. An equally attractive variety is *Hypericum Kalmianum*, which should be placed at the front of the border. Here both leaves and flowers are small and the flowers age gracefully and beautifully, the centres assuming a rich red-brown colour as they get older.

The double-flowered form of the Jew's Mallow, *Kerria*

*japonica flore pleno*, contrasts with the deep green of its heavily netted leaves, the round yellow rosettes of its many-petalled flowers. It grows very upright and will reach a height exceeding eight feet in favoured districts. The single-flowered variety has large flowers and is not so upstanding. Both varieties profit well by being pruned immediately after flowering.

The New Zealand Tea Tree, or manuka, *Leptospermum scoparium*, is one of the most attractive of early summer-flowering shrubs, which thrives in mild and maritime localities or in sheltered spots within the shrub border. The tiny green heath-like leaves are in certain of the varieties tinged with bronze, and *Leptospermum Boscawenii* with pale pink, small, five petalled flowers of great charm; *Leptospermum Chapmanii* with rose-red flowers, but the best of all is *Leptospermum Nichollii* with flowers of bright crimson. These may be safely, in the more severe localities, placed in the protection of backing and flanking conifers.

A charming plant is the bush honeysuckle, *Lonicera syringantha*, with its delightfully scented small clusters of lilac flowers, borne upon tangled bushes of arching strands generally about three to four feet in height; it is easily grown in any good garden soil.

MAGNOLIAS, in spite of their great beauty, are comparatively easy to grow in good deep soil in sheltered places, and though most varieties develop into quite large trees, many flower while they are quite small. They are so undeniably beautiful that they must be found a place in the shrub garden. The Chinese Yulan Tree, or *Magnolia conspicua*, is one such. It is deciduous, produces its large, cup-shaped, scented white flowers upon the bare stems in April, and though trees will reach a height in excess of thirty feet, they will flower when only three or four feet high.

*Magnolia conspicua*, when crossed with *Magnolia obovata*, which has heavily purpled flowers, gave rise to the *Soulangiana hybrids*, which are small trees or large shrubs and have goblet-shaped flowers, deeply stained with purple without. The variety *Magnolia Soulangiana* variety *Lenneii* has pale pink flowers similarly flushed.

But of all, the sweetest fragrance is dispensed by *Magnolia*

*Watsonii* with its huge flowers of immaculate white, with clustered crimson anthers around a sap-green style. This grows into a small tree like *Magnolia parviflora*, which is somewhat similar in appearance but which also flowers quite small.

*Magnolia stellata* is a slow-growing shrub with starry, semi-double scented white flowers produced upon the leafless branches in late March and early April. It is in every way worthy of a place in the shrub garden, and has a counterpart in *Magnolia stellata rosea*, with pale pink flowers.

All the Magnolias mentioned should be planted in sheltered places protected from the damaging rays of the early morning sun, and deserve the greatest care the gardener is able to bestow upon them.

The generic title MALUS, includes all the Apples known as the flowering crabs. *Malus floribunda* bears long, arching wands of crimson buds opening into clustered white flowers, and its variety *Malus floribunda atro-sanguinea* has a much more horizontally branching framework with clustered buds and flowers of rose-red. Developments of the wild Crab-Apple which sometimes add to the glory of their spring flowers the complement of brightly coloured autumn fruits (though it must be said that those which are most beautiful in flower seldom produce fruits) are *Malus Aldenhamensis*, with purple foliage, deep wine-red flowers, or Dartmouth, with large white flowers, and fruits showing a purplish bloom. John Downie with inverted pear-shaped fruits of orange and scarlet, and Veitch's scarlet with bright scarlet fruits.

The charm of *Osmanthus Delavayii* is contained, in part, in the neat, small, polished, deep evergreen foliage, and this conjunction is fortunate, since, until the shrub is mature, flowers are produced somewhat grudgingly. They are white, fragrant, and produced in small groups, resembling the flowers of lilac, with an elongated tube. Flowering in March, it earns a place in neutral soil.

PHILADELPHUS, the Mock Orange, is the Syringa of gardens. Syringa, to make confusion worse confounded, is the generic name for the Lilac of gardens. Of the genus PHILADELPHUS, selection confines itself to one species, *Philadelphus hybridus*, and to one variety, *Virginale*, which bears the largest double flowers and has the most delicate fragrance. All the hybrids are good. Generally the shrub attains a height of six feet and thrives even in the poorest of soils. For those who like neatness, *Manteau de Hermione* is trim and tidy, producing its creamy double flowers on bushes of about three feet. For those who detest double flowers, *Voie Lactée* has very large, striking single white flowers enhanced in beauty by golden stamens.

No shrub garden should omit representative Potentillas. All the varieties are subspecies of *Potentilla fruticosa*, which is very variable both in height and in the colour of its foliage, but each is easy to grow in almost any garden soil.

*Potentilla fruticosa Friedrichsenii* is an upstanding plant, reaching three feet in height, with green leaves and rather large pale yellow strawberry flowers.

*Potentilla fruticosa mandschurica* is a very dwarf silver-leaved variety with large, clear white flowers. *Potentilla fruticosa Farreri* has very neat small green leaves and produces its deep yellow flowers in profusion. *Potentilla Beesii* is a dwarf, has silver foliage, seldom grow more than a foot in height, and has large, deep yellow flowers.

*Potentilla Vilmoriniana* is taller, in fact much taller, sometimes more than four feet in height, but has creamy white flowers and is one of the best and most useful, adding this as if in full measure.

Of the genus PRUNUS, something at least has found its way into these pages, but one cannot resist the temptation to mention *Prunus Davidiana alba* which, planted with some protection unfalteringly produces its white flowers before all others, and seldom reaches more than nine feet in height. Nor should one miss *Prunus Sieboldii*, which is slow-growing and compact, seldom exceeding six feet in height, and produces semi-double rose-pink flowers closely clustered along the stems. For the small garden only *Prunus Sieboldii* (variety *Watereriana*) is better, for this has the typical growth of a dwarfed Japanese tree.

*Rhododendron* now includes *Azalea*, and opens up a vista of colour of a wideness of range unexcelled by any other species. But here the primary requirement for the grower is the correct type of soil. It must be free of lime. Where the texture of the soil is suitable—that is, where it is not a heavy marl, it can be treated in bulk with aluminium sulphate to render it acid, with good results. Fortunately the *Rhododendron* and *Azalea* are surface rooted, and Forrest chronicles instances where some of the species known to be completely calcifuge have been found growing in very shallow deposits of peat immediately super-imposed upon limestone.

It would be idle to suppose, however, that the would-be grower with a limy soil could dig out a hole, fill it with peat, plant a rhododendron, water it with hard limy water, and watch it go from strength to strength, rather would he see it decline and fall.

Upon a limy soil, beds must be built up in such a way that only the natural rainfall waters the bed, and assistance from the water-tap must be firmly eschewed. The ideal soil is a light peaty soil, slightly acid, or a light loam; heavy clays need lightening, and a correct gauge of the texture can be gathered from the feel of the sandy loam already indicated. A second requirement is a cool, moist root-run. Moisture can scarcely be brought to the Rhododendron, but ground cover can be pro-vided to ensure the coolness of the surface soil. The final require-ment is filtered sunshine, which can be contrived by siting it upon the north side of a taller planting, or in woodland positions which may vary from a few square yards to a much more extensive area. A north slope is very suitable, but is not essential where the district has a heavy summer rainfall.

In a chapter of this character it is quite impossible to do justice to the Rhododendron, but it is essential to point out the difference between some of the types. Earlier it was pointed out that the Azalea is now classed with Rhododendron, and the main point of difference is that the Azalea generally (but not always) bears bell-shaped flowers. The *Ghent Azaleas* (or honey-suckle-flowered Azaleas) are sweetly scented and vary in colour from white to blood-red. The crimson *Gloria Mundi* is typical of the group.

Of the mollis, and mollis and sinensis hybrids, Koster's Brilliant Red, and Anthony Koster are typical, but it is the Kersbergen strain which contains the most brilliant colours.

Among the species hybrids one finds also the dwarf Japanese forms of *Rhododendron indicum obtusum*, which again shade from

white to deep purple-crimson, keep neat in habit, and rarely
exceed two feet in height, bearing the typical colour masses in
such quantity as to daunt the eye.

Of the true species one may mention the giant *Rhododendron
barbatum*, often twenty feet in height, flowering as early as
February; *Rhododendron croceum*, with clear yellow bell-flowers
forming a tree of about six to eight feet in height; *Rhododendron
didymum* with a height of only two feet and with large blood-
red flowers; *Rhododendron moupinense*, flowering in March with
large, open blooms of white spotted with red, and not exceeding
two feet in height; *Rhododendron myrtilloides*, about twelve
inches in height, with its large, hanging bell-flowers produced
in pairs and of smoky claret, with a plum-like bloom upon them;
and *Rhododendron arboreum*, from which the many garden
hybrids have sprung. Mention must also be made of that
attractive variety, *Rhododendron cinnabarinum* with grey-green
foliage, which will exceed ten feet in height and which bears
large, hanging bell-flowers of soft cinnabar red, but of them
all my own especial favourite is *Rhododendron Wardii* with its
reddened buds, and cool soft yellow flowers, so adequately
pictured in Plate IX.

RIBES, or the flowering Currant, must not be neglected. Ever
ubiquitous, it provides one of the finest of town shrubs, and if
it is a case of no shrubs or Ribes, one can but prefer Ribes.
Unfortunately the kind usually grown in towns is confined to
*Ribes sanguineum*. Colour variations do exist, and *Ribes
sanguineum* variety *atro-rubens* has flowers of deepest red; *Ribes
aureum* has typical flowers of bright golden-yellow, and *Ribes
Gordonianum*, a hybrid between these species, is the most attractive of all, having flowers showing a combination of bronze-red
and yellow, with the netted foliage assuming most engaging
autumn tints, vying in beauty the earlier flowers.

Among my own personal favourites are the willows, particularly those of dwarf and symmetrical habit with heavily
silvered leaves. These are *Salix lanata*, with very round, very
woolly leaves of softly felted grey and upright catkins of bright
yellow. *Salix lapponum* is very similar and a hybrid of *Salix
lanata* with *Salix caprea* is slightly less grey, but none the less
has a great charm.

We cannot omit varieties of the species SALVIA. *Salvia Grahamii* given a sheltered position will delight the eye in the late autumn. Grown, as it can be, for the flavouring the sage leaves will impart to our food, it produces sprays of wide-lipped flowers of crimson-cerise, and it does this quite as well as it provides its searching aromatic odour. *Salvia azurea grandiflora* is similar and just as worth a place for its bright azure-blue flowers.

Can one miss such a plant as *Senecio Greyii*? True, its name indicates an affinity to the groundsel, but the silver foliage and large round golden flowers are so attractive in combination, and it is so easy to grow, that it must find a place. It grows to about four feet in height, and though large plants were killed in unprotected sites in January, 1941, smaller plants survived even that astonishing winter.

*Spartium junceum*—the Spanish Broom—is a really excellent plant for the back of the shrub border, reaching eight feet in height, with straight upstanding stems, clothed with large pea flowers of brightest gold from July to October. So easy to grow, it will persist long after every other plant has passed down the path to dusty death, scenting the air with its fragrance.

Moving still further down the alphabet, and drawing near to our conclusion, we come to *Spiraea*, and returning to the beginning of our alphabetic specifics, we reach *Spiraea arguta*, than which no flower can be whiter. The neat arching fronds are clad with clusters of small white flowers so impressive in the mass as to look frost-bespangled. The approximate height is about seven feet, but judicious pruning can give it less inches if required.

One of the best of the dwarf varieties is *Spiraea bumalda Anthony Waterer*, the long, deep green leaves of which make the perfect foil for its tabled heads of cherry-red. Seldom more than eighteen inches in height, it is an ideal shrub for the front of the shrub garden. *Spiraea japonica* has a similar appearance, but the flowers are of white, viewed through rose-coloured spectacles, which should be the colour of those worn by the gardener!

Progress leads us to SYRINGA—and that, as you will remember, is Lilac. When I first saw the species *Syringa tomentella*, I thought

I had found the most beautiful of the species. Strong in growth, its flower sprays are borne upon strong, upright stems, and each flower seems to be definitely articulated in that it stands out in clean separation from the others. The colour is pink and the scent is that of lilac; culture is as easy as for any other lilac and that, you will appreciate as you look around you, is just one small spot in which to grow.

*Syringa chinensis* is another favourite with its drooping heads of variable colour, which really doesn't matter, since all the grace in the world is contained in the symmetry of the careless wind-flung contour of the inflorescence.

But if your taste runs to solidity, or should it be stolidity, then you will prefer the more virile splashes of the double hybrid varieties *Madame Lemoine*—or the dark lavender of *Katherine Havemeyer*—or if you have a disregard for double flowers, the simplicity of the single white *Vestale*, or the more colourful *Souvenir de Louis Spath*, the sprays of which are claret and of a geometrical precision which just fails to be annoying. *Syringa Condorcet* has very large double, lilac flowers, and *Charles Joly* double, deep red flowers.

Pruning lilacs is a matter of removing the flowering heads just above the fork they form with the old wood. If you do this well, next year will be a little better for colour than was this!

Of the genus VIBURNUM, to which the well-known Guelder Rose, Snowball Tree or, to give it its full name *Viburnum opulus sterile*, belongs, four plants call for high honours. They are: *Viburnum Carlesii*, which is the most popular shrub of recent introduction; rarely exceeding four feet in height, it has a neat rounded outline and bears clusters of rose-pink buds which open to large heads of clear white flowers, carrying and spreading afar the characteristic scent of the *Carnation* in April! In autumn, to complete the cycle of beauty, the foliage brightens to red before it is cast. Growing well in most soils, it behaves with the utmost decorum if it is placed in a sheltered place, but please, not in isolation upon a windswept spot!

*Viburnum fragrans* rises a little higher; the specimen at which I am looking as I write reaches about eight feet. The buds are as rosy but are smaller, and in smaller clusters, but I have looked at them since November, and it is now February. The opened flowers are equally well-scented, and are clear white. The finely netted leaves when they are produced will add distinction to a shrub which has grace of shape in addition to its many virtues.

*Viburnum macrocephalum* is a great "snowball tree," the inflorescences of which can exceed eight inches in diameter. It is best placed in good soil against a sheltered wall.

For charm of form the variety *Viburnum tomentosum* variety *Mariesii* is outstanding. It stands about five feet high, its branches are produced laterally and horizontally to form a domed but flattened surface which is decorated by its entrancing snow-white clusters, the outer flowers of which are sterile and centred by a creamy, frothy inflorescence reminiscent of *Hydrangea Sargentiana*. The whole effect is that of a confection of a master magician.

And here one ends, conscious of many omissions, but also conscious of the fact that the selection contains in its scope varieties which cannot fail to give the pleasure which such beauty must pass on. He who plants a seed casts his eye into the future; he who plants a shrub, probes it deeply, but he who plants a tree has his eye upon the infinite.

# Chapter Twelve

## OF CLIMBERS

" 'Yes, but *I* grow at a reasonable pace,' said the Dormouse, 'not in that ridiculous fashion.' "

LEWIS CARROLL.

THE art of condensation should be the work of the scientist rather than of the gardener, for when the gardener attempts condensation in words, he is even more conscious of his limitations. This survey of climbing plants must therefore be regarded as an effort to remove most of the cream from the milk, rather than as a scientific condensation of it.

However appalling the thought of approaching the subject in alphabetical order may be, it has the advantage of at least being ordered, and so it shall be here again.

Thus at the beginning we come to *Akebia quinata*, which upon a south wall, in company with such elegant companions as *Rosa bracteata Mermaid*, above which climbs the majestic *Wistaria sinensis*, produces pale green, five-fold leaves that set off with artistry consummate, the deep purple female flowers produced in drooping clusters at the advent of spring.

*Berberidopsis corallina* is, mayhap, the most beautiful of all evergreen climbers, again needing the protection of a wall. Its dark green leaves form the fitting foil for its sprays of drooping coral-red flowers which fall in graceful arcs upon long, red-brown pedicels.

*Clematis montana rubens* is delightful with bronze leaves and soft pink flowers, and is at its best rambling through an inconspicuous shrub—*Clematis macropetala*, with its many-petalled flowers of lavender-blue, pendent like an enlarged Deutzia and followed by seed heads of silvery green, is even more fascinating than the Old Man's Beard, and for this reason is featured in Plate X. Nor can one forget the honey-scented *Clematis orientalis* or *tangutica*, as it is sometimes called, which will ramble through

an old tree and produce its four-petalled, golden-yellow drooping flowers and tasselled seed pots until the cold ingratitude of
winter's breath drives beauty back for another season.

Of the hybrid types (which you should ask to be "on their
own roots") *Lasurstern* is deep violet-blue and needs pruning
immediately it has completed flowering; *The President*, which
is dark plum-purple, can be pruned very heavily in the spring;
*Madame Marie Boisselot*, which has large white flowers, should
be only moderately pruned; it is similar in this respect to *Nellie
Moser*, which has very large flowers of pale mauve with a pink
stripe down the centre of each petal; *Jackmanii*, that very fine
old purple variety, can be vigorously pruned in the spring, for
it flowers on the new wood, the growth of which is definitely
encouraged by pruning.

*Eccremocarpus scaber* has curious feathery, pinnate leaves,
bears clusters of orange-scarlet tubular flowers, and deserves
the protection a south wall will afford. It will either climb or
trail along the ground, and adds distinction to either wall or
bank.

Of JASMINES, what may one find that is better than *Jasminum
nudiflorum*, whose scent enlivens many a winter day as it gleams
with borrowed sunshine? Yes, of course, *Jasminum primulinum*,
which with its evergreen foliage and semi-double flowers adds
just that touch of sophistication which adequate clothing can
give to such a charmer. A south wall is again indicated.

*Jasminum Beesianum*, which can climb to eight feet, has
purple-red flowers, attractive to those who like such colouring;
it is one of the parent of *Jasminum Stephanense*, which is vigorous,
hardy, and has fragrant pink flowers, freely produced.

If I pass by the genus LONICERA with but scanty notice, it is
not for their lack of beauty or of scent. It seems invidious to
choose from such a generously beautiful genus. *Lonicera
Brownii fuchsioides* has flowers of orange-scarlet and needs the
shelter of a south wall. *Lonicera japonica Halliana* has white
flowers which turn yellow, and *Lonicera tragophylla* has very
long tubes in outstanding clusters.

*Mandevilla suaveolens* has large white, sweetly scented flowers
produced in terminal racemes, and needs the protection of a
south wall.

12. Plagiorhegma dubium, a Japanese beauty

*Mutisia ilicifolia* is a climber also in need of a south wall, and produces large daisy flowers of deep rose, but is outshone by *Mutisia decurrens*, which has similar flowers of orange-scarlet with grey-green leaves and the benefit of additional hardihood.

*Solanum jasminoides*—related to the Potato—produces white potato flowers with protruding yellow centres, and should be sheltered on a south wall, where it will exert a charm upon the eye out of all keeping to that conveyed by its humbler relatives.

*Tecoma radicans* will reach twenty feet on a sheltered wall and its tubular orange-scarlet flowers in clusters are gay, or maybe gaudy, and appear so late in the year as to be twice welcome.

*Wistaria sinensis* has already had its mention. It is perhaps the most outstanding of all climbing plants. Grace, beauty, and complete elegance are so instinct in its person that few could cavil at its choice. The pendent sprays of deep mauve are freely produced when planted in good loam.

# Chapter Thirteen

## OF ALPINES

" 'Well, I should like to be a little *larger*, sir, if you wouldn't
mind,' said Alice; 'three inches is such a wretched height to
be.' "
" 'It's a very good height indeed,' said the Caterpillar angrily,
rearing itself upright as it spoke (it was exactly three inches
high)."

LEWIS CARROLL.

ALPINE plants contain among their number the pygmies
of the plant world. These are the little people, often the
inhabitants of high altitudes, which, like their human
counterparts, are either tractable and easy to accommodate or
difficult and pernickety, or under certain circumstances a mixture
of both. Probably the fascination of these little plants derives
some of its appeal from the innate desire in all of us to care for
the weak, but it does also in some part emanate from the instinct
in all of us to collect. In youth this is shown in some part by
the desire to acquire cigarette cards, regimental badges and the
like, and grows more mature in autographs and postage stamps.

Let it not be said, however, that this, to me the most interesting phase of all forms of gardening, deserves to degenerate into
collection merely for the sake of acquiring additional numbers
of botanical specimens. This can well be left to the Herbaria.

The Alpine Garden may be divided into four well-marked
sections comprising the rock structure, the scree, the Alpine
Meadow, and for want of a better name, the North slope. In
these features all plants may find suitable homes. Crevice plants,
that is those which in nature normally people the rock fractures,
and require in consequence a long cool root run, and find their
homes in the cracks between the rocks, in the rich vegetable
soil which the trapped decaying leaves eventually provide. The
scree provides an admirable medium for the plants which need

dry collars and a reasonable amount of moisture well below the surface; the North slope caters for the little fellows, to whom the sun in its fiercest array proves but an enemy in resplendent guise, and which prefer the somewhat more sober medium of filtered sunlight. The Alpine meadow is the medium by which the whole is brought into harmony with its surroundings, and is the home of those delightful charmers which, though small, devour space with an ever-increasing appetite, and strive among themselves for living room in which to unfold their beauty to the universe.

The beginner should try, as far as he is able, to keep these four sections firmly fixed in his mind, and while he may duplicate or reduplicate them within the scope of one complete entity which he may justly call his Alpine Garden, he should endeavour to plant and plan communities of plants of similar habit and spread, together, so that survival of individual varieties shall not be confined to those little people with the most gourmandising appetites for space.

I have no wish to try to condense within these few pages a complete guide to the art of growing Alpine plants, the task is impossible, as it would be to define what an Alpine plant is, since many plants figure in our Alpine gardens to-day which are "Alpine" solely by adoption, and indeed in my own garden many "Alpines" have degenerated into habits so vicious as to be as pernicious as weeds. Such a one is *Viola blanda*, a tiny white violet, with a face as calm and as peaceful as the moon upon a still and silent pool, and of charm so great, that it asks mutely to be spared! But spread far and wide it will, every seed germinates with the certainty usually ascribed to the tomato, but even worse, it runs with profusion underground, spreading far and wide, and deep too, in its search after sustenance. But it has serious rivals—in *Stachys lavandulifolia*—one of the family of nettles, with scented leaves, netted and hoary grey, with magenta flowers, barbarically set in grey festoons of tangled hairy bracts. Not too easy to keep alive in a small pot, it celebrates its release by running amok and is as hard to eradicate as couch grass—but much more lovely. But the premier award as a pest must surely fall to *Convolvulus althaeoides*—so lovely with its finely cut silver-grey leaves and huge nestling flowers of rich pink, and its long, deep roots—passing almost from pole to pole, in a way transcending the imagination of Jules Verne. The only advice one can give about such a plant is that it should be placed on a bank with a concrete wall on its north side, and a 20 foot road all round it. It is a comforting thought that someone somewhere, probably at the top of a basalt pillar in Fingal's Cave, finds it difficult to grow.

But these at least have beauty. Let us pass to such things as *Cotula squalida*—aptly named, which one can still find in lists, praised sometimes too, generally as what is called good bulb cover. This is a really rampageous plant which, placed in the interstices of crazy paving, will run with a speed almost incredible until every crack and cranny is packed tightly with its squalor; it will even contend with ground elder and live!

Another of this ilk is *Cerastium tomentosum*, which I once described in a catalogue—I am afraid much to the indignation of a few of my friendly correspondents—as "a rampant weed for which we are sometimes asked." This will honeycomb the earth with its white underground runners, and spread with the speed of a prairie fire—or at least, let us not exaggerate, at the rate at which a snail will travel towards a well-beloved plant! But with it all it has charm, and a garden I remember among those long since forgotten contained only two plants, this snow-white *Cerastium* and a creamy-pink *Heuchera* in equal masses

There are of course many plants to avoid, but generally every plant has its use, as my normal post bag always indicates, for I am quite sure that in spite of the very accurate description of the squalid enemy, at least one of my readers will write to know where it may be obtained, for it must be just the plant he has been searching for, for years.

These easily suited plants provide the criteria by which we should judge our success with others, for if we provide suitable conditions all the plants we love most should grow with equal fervour—a high standard indeed to set, and one completely unattainable, except maybe for those few things which will grow for each one of us as they will for no one else, but which by doing so provide us with inward satisfaction of having excelled at least in those. Just in fact like the old lady with the aspidistra!

13. Gentiana acaulis var. Collinsii

An exhaustive treatise upon Alpines cannot be expected to follow. I propose instead to deal with a limited number of personal favourites, and to place them in order of merit as it were, choosing a number of plants which I consider to be indispensible. First upon the list would come *Lithospermum diffusum* (*prostratum*) whose ability to spangle itself with stars of heavenly blue for long periods throughout the year, and literally to become a pool of blue at others, make it one of the most beautiful of all plants. It provides a constant source of income to the nurseryman from year to year, as it has the unaccountable habit of dying without apparent reason in some localities and soils. Where it is grown only with difficulty the gardener should try the effect of watering occasionally with a solution of 1 teaspoonful of Epsom salts (magnesium sulphate) to one gallon of water. Generally speaking it prefers a lime-free soil, but I strongly suspect that a magnesium deficiency is more likely to be responsible for its untoward passing.

The next favourite is *Gentiana sino-ornata*, introduced in 1917, I believe—I remember paying 7/6d. for my first plant—quite a tiny tuft. It proved at first quite difficult to grow until its needs were determined—namely a completely lime-free vegetable soil, composed either of leafmould or peatmould, or with a high humus content. In such a soil it thrives with satisfying celerity, so much that in October, 1939, I saw a field of half an acre which looked as if a giant with monstrous scissors had snipped out a patch of midsummer sky and let it fall upon the countryside.

Thirdly upon the list comes *Aethionema armenum Warley Rose*, a product of Miss Willmott's wonderful garden at Warley, and as satisfying a plant as ever graced a rock garden, growing into a wide, flat bush with small, tight heads of bright pink, like a diminutive Garland Flower. A better plant still is *Aethionema Mavis Holmes*, which has the blood of *Aethionema grandiflorum* in its veins, and whose finer, larger flowers are even more reminiscent of *Daphne Cneorum*. Both plants require a good garden loam in which to grow, and a place in the sun in which to thrive.

And now the order of merit rapidly begins to diverge so that it becomes rather like the family tree of the Plantagenets, for having placed the first three, choice becomes a matter of considerable thought and considerably less certainty. High in the list I would place *Phlox subulata*, variety *Camlaensis*, a product of that plant wizard the late F. W. Millard, so admirably pictured in Plate XI and couple with it the prostrate growing *Phlox Model*, whose lavender-pink flowers with deeper violet eyes are produced in flat swathes in the greatest prodigality. Both are exceptional plants, and as easy to grow in good garden soil in a sunny place as the *Aethionema*, and deserve a place in every rock garden.

The ubiquitous *Aubrieta* is the next plant, sometimes scoffed at by the tourist, but so colourful, that its expunction from the rock garden would be equivalent to prohibiting an artist from using coloured media. The outstanding *Aubrieta* is undoubtedly the variety *Gurgedyke*—raised I believe at the R.H.S. Gardens at Wisley. The individual flowers are not as large as some, but the colour is a rich, glowing purple, far deeper than any other; with it, and vying in splendour, is the rightly named *Magnificent*, probably the largest flowered of all, and of crimson magenta, as all the so-called *Red Aubrietas* are, with a distinctly deeper eye—a barbaric colour but very satisfying. Of the double red variety little need be said, except that when it first opens it is pink, and sometimes the flowers are not very double, but these little faults mend with time and it soon becomes an exceptionally attractive plant.

So far the plants mentioned are the quite ordinary kinds, seldom hard to grow and still less to obtain, and my more expert readers may be waiting for me to break into the fairyland of the more obscure Alpines, and not without justification, for some of the less well-known plants are indeed exceptionally beautiful. The so-called blue-eyed grass, or *Sisyrinchium bermudianum* is extremely beautiful, but it does not spread its seed far and wide and is transcended in beauty by another of similar appearance, but etherealized and beautified to such an extent as to provide a glamourised counterpart of the simple blue-eyed maiden! The beautiful stranger is *Aphyllanthes monspeliensis*, with rush-like leaves and wide petalled flowers of deeper, darker blue. Quite easily grown in good loam, it should be placed where the tender rush-like leaves are not nipped by the nimble fingers of frosts of the late spring, and then early in May the beautiful lass will open her wide blue eyes to gaze in wonder upon her protector. There exist at least two forms of this plant, both present in my own garden, one of which flowers with regularity, and the other which drags out a miserable existence and refuses to flower year after year. It is wise to take the precaution of obtaining plants of a good strain.

Another remarkable plant which must stand high in any order of merit is that fantastically named *Plagiorhegma dubia*, shown in Plate XII. Its curious rounded leaves which are cut at the tips in quaint fashion, but when the plant flowers are scarcely in evidence. The deep lavender blue flowers change colour as they age, and are reminiscent of the Anemone, but are borne in such profusion that they arrest the attention, and what is still better, continue to hold it. *Plagiorhegma dubium* is a native of Japan and thrives best in a shady place in a soil which is light but leafy.

Of all DIANTHUS, *Dianthus caesius*, a native which long since decorated the steep, sunny faces of the Cheddar Gorge, and which in recent years could be found almost anywhere else, is still among my foremost favourites, for it combines with the attraction of its fringed pink open-faced flowers, the scent characteristic of the Carnation, in quantity sufficient to be overpowering upon a bright shining day, and for once one must not complain of the not overpainted but over-perfumed lady!

*Dianthus alpinus* has the charm of greater sophistication in its array, but is a little more discreet in its perfume. Its tiny stems and deep brown buds are suitable preparation for the production of its round, fringed, deep pink flowers, ringed in the centre with a heavily speckled carmine band. It thrives quite literally in sharply drained loam, rich in humus, but exhibits a more becoming modesty in the austere conditions of the scree. A hybrid, *Dianthus Boydii*, is a longer-lived plant, but any pinch of seed of *Dianthus alpinus* will produce sufficient variations in form and colour to delight the plants man.

The adverse criticism applied to most rock garden plants seems centralised about their prepondering penchant to flower in the spring, and in the spring only. Such criticisms are of course a sweeping generality, and *Zauschneria* excludes itself. If I recollect aright the discoverer of *Zauschneria microphylla* was startled to see in the far distance, high up in the mountains, a large patch of what appeared to be sealing-wax red. A long climb brought her to a vast expanse of this Andean beauty. *Zauschneria microphylla* under garden conditions can border upon the rampant varieties and runs underground in a hot dry spot with rapidity, but in the waning summer comes to reward, for, spaced with deft artistry upon the green-grey wands, fall the slender tubular flared flowers, like scarlet cornucopias, pouring their richness upon a barren soil, and continuing so to do until the rude winter refuses such bounty. *Zauschneria californica* is less wild and has larger and greener leaves, lacks the windflung grace of its relative, but shares its preference for the autumn.

What can I select among the Saxifrages? For grace, undoubtedly *Saxifraga Cotyledon montavonensis*, the flowers of which fit the curving spires so well that one would deny the artist the right to paint out even one. The individual flowers lack the solidity of those of *Saxifraga longifolia* variety *Symons Jeuneii*, the flower sprays are shorter, but—well, let us put them together into the garden and decide another time. For those of you who prefer a more flaunting beauty I can strongly recommend *Saxifraga Cotyledon caterhamensis*, the flowers of which are so heavily speckled with red that they confuse the retina and it registers pink! All these silver saxifrages are devoted to cracks and crannies with quite a lot of sun to fall upon their faces.

The pygmies of the genus are found in the Kabschia section, and it would be a brave man who would confine his selection to one variety only. Of the deep pink flowered varieties *Saxifrage Cranbourne* is so reliable that it selects itself. Of pale pink varieties *Saxifrage Irvingii* gives me greater pleasure than *Saxifrage Jenkinsii*, both of which are exceptionally good. Of the whites *Saxifrage Burseriana crenata* whose quaintly cut petals give it an air which none of the other varieties succeeds in capturing. Among the yellow flowered varieties *Saxifrage Faldonside* still retains its claim to extravagant praise. All these varieties should be planted in the scree, preferably a high scree, or better still in a trough lifted so high that even the tallest among us should not have to bend his back, or push his spectacles up, to peer at their myriad of beauties. The plutocrats may house them in Alpine Houses, and the less blessed protect them with sheets of glass propped over their heads upon pieces of wire or sticks, against the heavy February rains, which bring with them also the power to bleach and otherwise spoil, but there does come upon occasion a February such as visits our islands once in a decade, when the daring gardener, hardened by at least seven years of waiting, at last sees a giant plant unspoiled by rain or snow or frost or slugs or snails, burst into flower, growing in the open, and all the disappointments of the past are repaid, while those of the future have no significance. Much controversy has taken place upon the cultural requirements of the *Kabschia Saxifrages*. A correspondent once blamed me for the death of the bulk of his specimens, because in one of my published works I recommended fully sunny conditions in the scree, with copious water in hot dry spells, but later admitted that he had never "bothered" to water them. In my own garden they thrive in an ash scree, facing south, with a maximum of sun, but are never allowed to be short of water in the summer. In the main, however, it is easier for the amateur to be content with a little less characteristic growth, and the added safety entailed by planting in position facing southwest, but the prime needs of summer moisture and winter dryness should not be forgotten.

One always hesitates to "puff" varieties which one has raised oneself, and my next three selections I advance with some diffidence mixed with a great deal of pride.

First and foremost I would place *Gentiana acaulis* variety *Collinsii*, which originated as a seedling of *Gentiana acaulis* and shows brilliant blue, open-faced flowers in much profusion, with little of the shyness of certain forms of *Gentiana acaulis*, whose tardiness in flowering is said to be of bacterial origin, and *Gentiana Collinsii*, which I selected for Plate XIII, seems to be immune. But its greatest claim to recognition is the width of the petals and plicae which are much bolder than those of *Gentiana acaulis*, and it will I think soon become both well known and popular.

The second plant is *Saponaria ocymoides* variety *rubra compacta*, which is an extraordinarily tight growing, deep rose pink form of *Saponaria ocymoides*—a soapwort which takes up immeasurable space. The offspring does not show this fault, and literally becomes a tight mat of dense, deep colour in May. The plant received an unanimous award of merit of the Chelsea Flower

Show in 1939 and is a really exceptional plant. Certain forms
—not of the original strain—fail to reach the standard set by
the first plant, failing to exhibit the same depth of colour, and
produce larger but thinner petalled flowers which detract largely
from its charm. The original plant has one fault common to
all Saponarias—it has no long life, but it can be kept going
from cuttings which should be taken in June. Professor Brooks
at the Botany School at Cambridge tells me that he has produced
seedlings which are true both to colour and type; my own seed
almost invariably produces something quite different, so I keep
a young stock constantly going by vegetative means.

The third plant is a deep but glowing red form of *Anemone
Pulsatilla*, which I have called Eva Constance, which is of the
parentage *Anemone Pulsatilla rubra x Anemone Pulsatilla Mrs. Van
der Elst*, and again does not breed true from seed, though it is
possible that we shall yet accomplish this desired result. At the
moment it is extremely hard to produce, since the only means
of ensuring a true strain is from root cuttings, which take a
number of years to mature into reasonable plants. The fortunate
possessors of the few flowering plants which have been allowed
to leave here, are all enthusiastic about it, and it is a source of
great satisfaction to know that a single plant nursed with almost
superhuman care for seven years, is at last producing others of
its kind, and will soon spread throughout many gardens to give
as much pleasure as the original gave me when it first unfolded
its lovely petals in a jumble of mediocrity.

High in any list of Alpines I would place *Polygala calcarea*, a
variative of the Common Milkwort, which in almost any good
soil forms a mat of rounded deep green leaves and small flowers
of two shades of blue, which suggest exotic moths with much-
frilled multiple antennæ, produced in such profusion that the
foliage is completely obscured. This plant rarely exceeds two
inches in height, and is I think outstanding among the pygmies.

Another plant small in stature, but with the major appeal of
the tinies, is *Erigeron uniflorus*, a tiny many-petalled pink daisy
on a stem of about an inch. The specific name implies that it has
one flower on a stem—not one flower to each plant—and a large
plant, if you are fortunate enough to possess one, is a source of
envy to your neighbours, and of undoubted pride of possession.

Of PRIMULAS I have three vastly dissimilar favourites. *Primula denticulata Hay's variety* is named after that wonderful gardener Mr. Tom Hay, V.M.H. The soft lavender of the ordinary toothed primrose yields to a deeper almost violet blue in the case of this Primula, and the strengthened colour adds greatly to its charm. The second is *Primula helodoxa*, which raises its circular tiers of buttercup yellow flowers upon slender but strong stems, and scents the air with its fragrance. It is most at home in a damp soil, preferably in the neighbourhood of a pool in which the tall tiers are reflected in the water in the company of the calm stately beauty and sombre leaves of the waterlily which forms the subject of Plate XIV and which forms, I think, a fitting close to a remarkable series of pictures.

The final Primula is one of easy growth called *Sir Bedivere*, and is of the Juliana type, with deep maroon red flowers, starry in shape, but produced in such astonishing abundance that it can on no account be omitted from the garden.

A selection of Alpines which omitted the *Campanula* would be damned indeed! These relatives of what we Sassenachs have called the Harebell, but which to the Scots is the Bluebell of Scotland, have the direct simplicity, and the generosity of these same Scots, and this is no small praise as any Englishman who has experienced Scots hospitality will well know. When however we come to place them in a set order of merit we meet a problem to which the answers are as satisfactory as those of a quadratic equation with imaginary roots.

Running where angels fear to tread, I suggest that pride of place is the probable prerogative of *Campanula Avalon*, a hybrid of *Campanula turbinata* and *Campanula Raineri*, and the main reason is that the discerning people of Liverpool acquire this as soon as they see it, and leave so little to be absorbed by the rest of the country that it must indeed be good! But you may think that the Liverpudlian desire for a good bargain may be an insufficient reason for you to follow blindly. *Campanula Avalon* is a dwarf, seldom, if ever, exceeding four inches in height, and has large open cup-shaped flowers of deep violet blue, and runs in any good open soil to form a tuft of grey green leaves with certainty and speed, so that in the course of a single year the small original plant will occupy at least a square foot. Flowering in late July and early August it is as desirable as it is beautiful.

Nor can one leave out *Campanula arvatica*, in size but a poor relation, and which runs with similar rapidity, vying with the Speedwell in its capacity to devour space. In late June this little fellow puts into a background of small bright green leaves, its open violet stars, spangling its carpet with a flowering counterpart of the Milky Way. If you find that it grows with such profusion that disposal becomes imperative, your friends will welcome the plant's generosity.

A plant with a chequered history is *Campanula lasiocarpa*, which came from N.W. America with a tale of difficulties, but which proved so tractable, so prolific, and so easy to propagate from the seed which it produces with spendthrift generosity, that in spite of all the difficulties, troubles, and trials of severe winters, mild winters, wet winters, and dry winters, it still remains with us. For a light, well-drained soil nothing could be more apposite than its notched lettuce green leaves, and ribbed, solid petalled flowers of soft lavender blue, borne upon short, fleshy, green stems in late June.

Finally, among the Campanulas I would select *Campanula Rainerii*, whose open goblets of milky blue are kept aloft as if to catch the nectar of the gods, for the benefit of such celestial visitors who may find the beauty of the prospect irresistible. It calls for scree treatment.

A small and dainty charmer is *Globularia cordifolia* variety *bellidifolia*, which forms a compact mass of evergreen polished leaves, shaped like those of the common daisy, secluding in their depths the rounded blackish buds which will, in May, lengthen their stems by an inch or so, and widen their heads into small spherical "powder puffs" of grey blue. It would be hard to deny it the little space it will normally grace in soil which is not too rich or too heavy.

A companion not the least overshadowed, overborne, or outgrown by the latter is *Armeria caespitosa*, which forms a similarly rounded tuft of neat wiry grass-like foliage, and displays upon stems of insignificant length, fellow flowers of pale pink. These are two of a kind, fitted by habit and domicile to everlasting association.

14. "In the pool, besides the Lilies, are reflected the colours of the
Candelabra Primulas"

Of *Sedums* and *Sempervivums* one could write without end, but who would care to choose between the bright green and crimson fleshy leaves of *Sedum caeruleum*, overborne by an effervescence of starry, clear pale blue flowers, and *Sedum pulchellum*, the neat orderliness of whose geometrically patterned, slender, pale green leaves, is additionally marked by the red brown tips, and overshadowed by the huge starfish of deep pink flowers. True *Sedum caeruleum* is an annual; it does, however, produce such quantities of seed that one plant ensures its own succession, after flowering, with even greater application and industry than is met with in any of its kind.

There runs a legend, and who shall say that it is only that, that the house that is honoured by the presence of the house-leek upon its roof, will never be struck by the fangs of lightning. That Thor should be so discerning should prove of great satisfaction to those who fear the wrath of Jove ! Beauty and symmetry combine in the genus SEMPERVIVUM more exactly than in any other.

*Sempervivum Schlehanii* is the gem of the genus, forming huge rosettes of deep red, tipped and edged with green, and fringed with lashes like the lovely eyes of a languishing lady, sprung to stardom from obscure poverty. Given the slightest nourishment *Sempervivum Schlehanii* will live, but given a little more and copious water to drink in summer, it waxes in size and assumes its most gorgeous appearance when drink is at last withheld. Its flowers comprise but the least of its beauties, and are red, margined with white, and the seed which follows—because of its promiscuity—germinates like cress. Plate XV introduces one to the patterned and colourful beauties.

But if beauty is to be judged by length and prodigality of cilia, all competitors must retire at the advent of *Sempervivum ciliosum*, a small, pale pea green, rosetted plant with such hosts of filaments of silver that it appears heavily webbed or frosted. In addition it has attractive yellow flowers which appear at yearly intervals if the immature rosettes are kept sufficiently dry during the winter.

The cobwebbed houseleek *Sempervivum arachnoideum* has no compere in beauty when planted in a rock crevice, where it will turn itself to the happy task of adding innumerable rosettes in the neatest precision until there remains no further space to fill, when it will overflow over rock face and spill itself wherever a crack provides roothold.

One still supports in old age the childish habit of retaining a titbit until the last, and though high praise has been given to all the previously mentioned species, my own especial favourite is without doubt *Sempervivum erythraeum*, of neatly patterned, short, wide, pale purple grey leaves, dusted as with a soft farina, with microscopic white hair. The flowers are remarkably fine, being of reddish purple with a central white zone in each of their twelve petals.

For the man with a garden only of tiny dimensions no plants can give more satisfaction than the *Sempervivums*. Of easy culture, of almost legendary indestructibility, of constant variation, individually, and of immense range collectively, they deserve the attention of the amateur specialist to a degree which few other plants can ask, and would be admirable companions for the gardener wrecked upon a desert island, since they possess that intrinsic beauty which cannot pall, and which does not age, and completely lacks the monotony of immutability.

America has surely given the garden no greater gift than the PENTSTEMONS, or if you wish, the PENSTEMONS. The criterion I apply in selection is the relativity of ease of growth with the incidence of colour, and I would place here as the most outstanding *Pentstemon rupicola* (this is the *Pentstemon Roezlii* of catalogues). The neat, rounded, grey-green leaves ornament a tightly compacted shrub of about half a foot in height, and in May are bedecked with sprays of bright rose-crimson tubular flowers. Thriving in a hot dry soil, and easy to propagate from its freely produced cuttings, *Pentstemon rupicola* is the most satisfying of the family, though it has competitors of a high order in *Pentstemon Scoulerii* with large lilac-blue flowers, and *Pentstemon Davidsonii* with flowers of deep lilac.

Of the genus VERONICA I shall select but two plants. One is *Veronica armena*, a prostrate growing plant with little finely cut leaves, which sit neatly upon the ground, sometimes rising a little on the stronger stems, but which are submerged by the mass of Gentian blue flowers which are so freely produced in May, and thence onward throughout the year, when given the sunny aspect and good light soil it seems to love. A gem, too, is *Veronica canescens*. *Veronica filiformis* takes one's breath by its beauty, but monopolises one's time to eradicate. *Veronica canescens* will run as quickly, but its runners and its leaves are but as coating of frost upon the ground. Then, one day in June, the surface of the soil seems to become spangled with pale blue milky stars which sit upon it like a galaxy in a grey firmament, and upon each successive day the pattern changes, until at long last the heavenly show is over, to return again only with the coming of another season.

It would be difficult indeed to omit one of the genus OENOTHERA, but here certainly I misdoubt my ability to confine the selection to a single species. Shall it be *Oenothera missouriensis* with its gigantic saucer-like flowers of clear yellow borne upon a galumphing plant, which earns this right by the clarity and purity of its colour? Less than a foot in height, its triumphal progress carries it over a large space in a single season, but when winter comes, its leaves and stems pass away, only to be still more strongly renewed by the spring which follows.

In direct contrast is the sedate, and incredibly neat *Oenothera pumila* which bears its small four-petalled flowers in the leaf-axils of a small-leaved slender stemmed plant, which seldom exceeds nine inches in height. A companion as pleasant and as neat, but with larger flowers of deep pink is *Oenothera mexicana*, seldom seen in cultivation but with a temperament its place origin would seem to belie. Both plants flower for a long period and do well in a sunny spot in good garden soil.

One can close no selection of attractive and popular Alpines without a selection of VIOLAS. Here I would place first *Viola striata*—another American—with very large clear white " violets" with the basal and dorsal petals heavily pencilled with deep violet blue. The large typical violet leaves form a fit setting for the very beautiful flowers and the easy culture of the plant which grows either in sun or shade, make it a paramount selection.

The Rouen violet, *Viola rothomagensis*, is a tiny pansy with deep lilac flowers which is as busy as a bee. As a rule it flowers first in February and indefatigably pursues its chosen path until the coming of winter enforces a brief rest. The flowers are small but they are produced with freedom, so that this is indeed a plant for free men.

And finally to end the selection, a native plant, *Viola biflora*. This is a plant for a shady spot, which runs with underground thickened stems, produces freely, fertile seed, and generally brightens the spring with its butter yellow flowers, fashioned like those of the wood-violets, borne two at a time in the green leaf axils. This is definitely not a plant for the sunny places, it does not flaunt but creeps as insidiously into the consciousness as it does through the shady nooks it graces, to persist both in the one and in the other. I hope it will be your favourite too.

At the end of such a selection one is conscious that there are many omissions, but one need not I feel make them the subject of an apology. Those of you who already love these things, will appreciate some of the little people you have already met, but will be left with an unexplored field of discovery in which you may roam at will, with the prospect of more and pleasant surprises.

Those who disdain the keen rock-gardener as a crank should try to beg a plant or two from their friends, particularly of the varieties mentioned. They will then soon be fascinated by a phase of gardening which presents problems beyond the ordinary, and exacts a high measure of intelligence and skill from its followers, for their solution.

15. Sempervivums, aristocratic relatives of the Houseleeks

# Chapter Fourteen

## OF VEGETABLES

"The great question certainly was, what? Alice looked all round her at the flowers, and the blades of grass, but she could not see anything that looked the right thing to eat or drink under the circumstances. There was a large mushroom growing near her, about the same height as herself; and when she had looked under it, and on both sides of it, and behind it, it occurred to her that she might as well look and see what was on top of it.

She stretched herself up on tiptoe and peeped over the edge of the mushroom, and her eyes met those of a large blue caterpillar, that was sitting on the top, with its arms folded, quietly smoking a long hookah, and taking not the slightest notice of her or of anything else."

LEWIS CARROLL.

THE basis of production of good vegetables is intelligent cultivation. This implies that the gardener takes into consideration every known factor with regard to his "native soil."

Light soils, that is, soils which dig easily and which are not necessarily lighter in weight or in colour, naturally present a different problem from those which are heavy or dig with difficulty. But the primary aim is the same, no matter what the initial texture of the soil may be, and that aim is to produce what we may call a well-balanced soil.

Any attempt to alter the texture of the soil is dependent upon digging, and though recent research suggests that digging of some types of soil may be overdone, there is no substitute if it is necessary to incorporate new constituents to effect a change of texture. Nor is it possible to omit digging where it is necessary to use the agency of sun and frost to help to alter it.

Digging appears to the uninitiated to be so simple that most of its best professional exponents have been the lowest paid but the highest primary producers in the world. Their reward has been mainly confined to their good fortune in indulging an occupation which is so healthy and so near to nature, that nature has been left to provide for them. Digging can scarcely be called irksome, for it provides no great strain upon mental processes and brings in its train the satisfaction characteristic of all forms of manual work.

But to return to the soil. Light soils, which are generally also early soils, retain little moisture and need heavy dressings of manure or of any material which will retain moisture, such as leaves, or rotting vegetable material.

Heavy soils require the addition of any material which will help to expedite drainage, such as sand, ash or grit, and if it is possible to incorporate such ingredients as chopped straw, old thatch or similar material, this will bring about the required consistency with speed. It may be said that generally speaking all soils require that treatment which will reduce any excess of the main constituent. It should be made quite clear, however, that the clay constituent of the soil contains all the inorganic matter necessary to the life of the plant in the most finely divided form, in which it is most readily available to the plant, and all efforts and cultivation must tend to make these inorganic constituents easily available.

The addition of lime to heavy clay soils causes the adherence of particles and renders the soil more granular, adding as a corollary better drainage; but the application of lime also helps in balancing and rendering available to the plant the phosphorus already present in the soil. Where the soil already contains sufficient lime for this purpose the addition of further lime does not add to its fertility.

A brief survey of those vegetables which the gardener may desire to grow now seems appropriate. One of these is the globe artichoke, which can hardly be called a profitable crop, but it has the advantage of being as attractive in the border as upon the dinner plate. "Green globe" is probably the best variety and should be grown from seed sown in a hotbed in March, hardened off in May, and planted out. In the second year runners may be detached from the old plants and planted in rows four feet apart, with three feet between the plants. If grown in the border, it should be placed well to the back. The edible part is the immature flower bud which should be well washed in salt water before cooking, and cooked in boiling water for about half an hour. The stems and leaves are also blanched and used as saladings.

The Jerusalem artichoke—the name is a corruption of *Girasole d'Articiocco*—is also quite ornamental at the back of the border, but it is one of the vegetables richest in protein. Its somewhat earthy flavour is not appreciated by some, but this is not so noticeable when eaten raw, as the ingredient of a salad. It is one of the easiest of all vegetables to grow, needing little attention in good dry soil. The seed tubers are planted four inches deep, 15 inches apart, in rows three feet apart, preferably in October, or failing that, in March. They should be cooked in water to which a little vinegar has been added, and where the earthy flavour is distasteful an added onion will give palatability. Storage should be in large boxes with a layer of ashes at the bottom and then alternate layers of tubers and ashes. The final layer of ashes should be covered with straw, but the tubers should be kept outside and not allowed to become dry, for frost will not harm them; they also provide an appetising dish for slugs, and this protection will save them from the results of such excessive affection.

The Broad Bean has an undeserved unpopularity. It is exceptionally nutritious, stores well, and is suited particularly to heavy soils, but in light soils a heavy mulching of grass cuttings is advisable in the spring. The autumn sowing of Broad Beans in the South is generally recommended, but my own experience is that if the beans are well soaked beforehand, an early March sowing is likely to be quite as early in cropping. The pest most likely to affect the bean is the black aphis or Collier. Watch carefully for its onset, pick out the tops of the plants immediately and burn them. A bad spring for this pest can often be anticipated in the country by an examination of the spindle-berry in winter. Collier hibernates thereon, and if the spindle-berry is clear one may hope for a year when the pest will not be prevalent. After the first crop cut the plant back to the ground and you will certainly get another crop. The beans should be planted in double rows, the beans staggered with four inches between the beans and four inches between the rows. The double rows should have two feet between them. Beans to be stored should be gathered young, shelled, blanched in boiling water for five minutes, rinsed in cold water, and thoroughly dried in the sun. Store them in bags. Dried beans should be soaked for twelve hours before cooking, which is done by boiling for not longer than thirty minutes in well-salted water.

Brown Dutch Beans are the type of Haricot bean well suited for storing and easily grown upon well-drained soil. They should be planted in the same way as Broad Beans but with six inches between the beans in the double rows and two feet between the rows. The pods should stay upon the haulm until they are fully ripe, and be completely dried in the sun, after which they may be stored in bags. They should be soaked for at least twelve hours before cooking. They make an admirable and nutritious addition to soups, and may be used with chopped carrots as filling for pasties as a meat substitute.

Dwarf French Beans, or Kidney Beans, are very prolific, store well, and are available from early August to November. Two of the best varieties are Canadian Wonder, and Masterpiece, which are sown similarly to the Haricots from early May onwards. Waxpod Beans are grown similarly. A sowing made as late as August 1st, produced a really exceptional and acceptable crop which was finally picked on November 11th. Germination is quicker if the seeds are well soaked before planting. French Beans should be picked while young and tender and cooked whole for twenty-five minutes in boiling water. They may be grown, however, as haricots and the seed dried, stored, and similarly used. The simplest method of storage is to pick the beans while young, blanch them for five minutes in boiling water, and wash immediately in cold water. They should then be dried in a slow oven until they become brittle, when they may be stored in any air-tight container. Before using they should be soaked until their early softness returns.

The Runner Bean would, if it was not edible, be grown for the attractions of its astonishingly beautiful, scented flowers. It is a half-hardy perennial, and the roots can, if they are lifted before severe frosts, be dried and stored in a dry frost-proof place. On the whole, however, it is best to raise each season's plants from new seed, which should be grown in deeply-dug soil which has been dressed with wood ash but has not been too heavily nor too freshly manured. A good plan in light soils is to dig in all the available grass clippings before planting the seed. Seeds should be planted in staggered rows with nine inches between the seeds, and the rows should be three feet apart. Beans should be gathered young and thinly sliced from end to end, boiled in salted water for twenty to twenty-five minutes; to be stored they should be gathered similarly and treated exactly as recommended for French Beans.

An attractive variation is the Painted Lady bean, with yellow pods attractively streaked with cerise-red. It looks quite too Oriental to be eaten with safety, but it is as smooth to the palate as it is amazing to the eye.

Beet is a vegetable with a high food value, which stores well, but is seldom grown in sufficiency or cooked as it deserves. It should be preferably grown in rich soil, well dug. "Patch-sowing" in May in groups of from three to four seeds in spots about six inches apart, with the drills one inch deep and one foot apart is the easiest and most economical method. All but the strongest seedlings in each patch are eliminated later. Care should be taken when the hoe is used that the roots of the plants are not cut, or they will bleed; similarly at lifting time the same care should be exercised to see that the roots are undamaged. The leaves should be screwed off and not cut off for the same reason. The best varieties are Blood Red and Cheltenham Green Top in the long-rooted kinds—which are best for keeping—and Empire Globe and Crimson Ball in the globe-rooted kinds.

Boiled beetroot as a cold dish is too well known to need description, but the flavour of the beetroot is much improved if it is baked instead of boiled. This method is also a good one for preparing beetroot as a hot dish, when it should be served with a vinegar or horse-radish sauce.

Broccoli resembles the Cauliflower in some respects but is much hardier, and with appropriate care can be produced in succession almost throughout the year. There are three types, one of which closely resembles the Cauliflower, Star Broccoli, which produces up to nine small but characteristic "curds," and sprouting Broccoli, of which the edible parts are the sprouting heads, which are incredibly useful owing to their intensely hardy nature, and their persistence into late March and early April.

The seed of all varieties is quite small and light, over 1200 seeds comprising each ounce.

As a rule firm and heavy, but well-dug soil is the best medium, and a slow-acting fertiliser like hoof-and-horn meal is the best. The crop takes between nine and twelve months to mature and sowings should be made with the idea of providing a succession throughout the whole year. In the warmer south, the five Roscoff varieties undoubtedly cover the whole of the year, and a selection from Winter White, Springtide, Early Feltham, Late Feltham and Veitch's Self-Protecting will cover the Autumn and Winter; Leamington is useful for the Spring, and Veitch's Model or Late Queen provide the later varieties.

Seed should be sown—with protection if necessary—out of doors in March for crops to mature in the Autumn; in April for crops which it is desired to have ready for winter use, and in late April or May for Spring crops. When the plants are large enough, they should be transplanted in rows two feet apart, with two and a half feet between the ranks.

As Broccoli introduces the Brassicas it would be as well for a while to regard some of the pests which are incident to the whole family. These number, among others, the Cabbage Root Fly, which lays its eggs on the soil near the stem, and is best discouraged with a proprietary brand of Calomel dust. Caterpillars are best hand-picked under small garden conditions, and care should be taken to crush the patterned egg deposits upon the leaves; alternatively derris can be used as a spray. The Cabbage Aphides, which in bad cases form colonies of dense grey-green flies, can be among the worst of the pests, and badly infested plants must be burned, while plants less affected should be dusted with a nicotine and pyrethrum powder. Cabbage White Fly can be controlled by a nicotine spray. The Leather-jacket, or grub of the Cranefly or Daddy-longlegs, which works upon the stem just under the surface of the soil can usually be detected by the flaccidity of the leaves, and should be searched for and destroyed. Flea Beetle often attacks seedlings of the Brassicas but can be controlled with dustings of derris or pyrethrum powder, but if the attack of the beetle is delayed until the seedling plants are large, most plants will not be unduly affected by it. Gall Weevil can be distinguished by the characteristic white but soft swelling in the stem and can be noticed in the seedlings. When planting out, the gall should be cut away and the grub destroyed, or the plants burned.

The three diseases of fungoid origin which attack the Brassicas are Downy Mildew, White Blister, and last and most important, Club-Root. The first two can be stamped out by drenching the soil with Bordeaux mixture, and the first signs are shown by the greeny-yellow colouration of the leaves in the case of Downy Mildew, and in White Blister by the curious blistering of the leaves.

Club-Root is the most serious of the diseases, and prevention must be aimed at, since there is no cure. Liming the soil well, will do much to prevent the onset of the disease, which makes its presence obvious by the hard swelling which appears on the stem and root, which will cause the plant to flag in warm sunshine. All affected roots should be burnt and none of the Brassica family should be grown upon the same ground for several years.

Another Brassica is the Brussels Sprouts, a crop which takes well over six months to mature, and, provided the young plants are got into position early in the year, is best grown in firm, undug limed ground, and fed with a little sulphate of ammonia at fortnightly intervals. If you are not prepared to feed regularly with artificials, the ground should be well dug and manured before planting. Soot may be dusted around the plants to protect them from slugs. Each plant is put in with a trowel with a handful of prepared soil, and left to work out its own destiny. To produce the young plants sow the seeds in a cold frame in March, transplant once and then set out in position in ranks two and a half feet apart each way, in May.

I must confess that the finest specimen of Brussels Sprouts I ever possessed grew itself. A dropped seed fell into a 3-in. pot which normally would have housed a small flowering plant. By intense application to its task it grew into the tallest, heaviest and most perfect specimen of its kind I have yet seen, dwarfing its carefully planted and cossetted fellows—possibly to show that the hand of chance still plays the major part in "the best laid schemes o' mice and men."

A variety strongly recommended is Cambridge No. 5; others are Wroxton, Paris Market, Fillbasket, and Clucas's Favourite.

The Cabbage is the easiest of all vegetables to grow, the most important of the Brassicas, and provides green food all the year round for both the family and the garden pest. The Cabbage likes a good fertile but firm soil. The spring Cabbage should certainly follow the Potato crop, and should not be grown each year upon the same site.

The best Spring varieties are: Flower of Spring, Harbinger, Ellam's Early Market, and Offenham and Carter's Velocity.

The autumn varieties are: Winnigstadt, Wheeler's Imperial, Primo, Christmas Drumhead, and All the Year Round.

The spring-maturing varieties should be sown in seed-beds in July and transplanted into ranks one and a half feet apart, and with one foot between the plants, in September. For the autumn-maturing crop sowings should be made in April and transplanting should take place in May in rows two feet apart, with a foot and a half between the plants.

Varieties with small, tight round heads,—Carter's Velocity is typical—are usually quick in maturing, taking about thirteen weeks from sowing to maturity, and have no waste. Sown in gentle heat in March, Carter's Velocity can be planted out in early May and cut in late June. This should be planted, for this purpose, in rows fifteen inches apart and with twelve inches between the plants. Plant very firmly. There are between six hundred and seven hundred seeds to one ounce of Cabbage seeds.

Red Cabbage should be treated as an autumn-maturing variety, and the gardener should not disdain to cook it as an ordinary cabbage, as it is extremely palatable when boiled or braised, after having been well shredded, and its beauty, as caught in Plate XVI, should not be overlooked.

The Carrot is a crop which can be available for about eight months of the year; it stores well and has a high food value, and grows best in loose, light loam which has been well dug, but not freshly manured, worked into a finely divided consistency, and fertilised with two ounces of superphosphate of lime and one and a half ounces of hoof-and-horn meal per square yard.

The best long-rooted varieties are: Scarlet Horn and Improved Early Horn (at intervals from April onwards). The seeds should be sown in drills twelve inches apart and thinned to four inches apart; seed will often germinate unevenly, but usually as hope departs the carrot comes into evidence. One ounce of seed will cover a one hundred and fifty foot run. The worst pest is the Carrot Fly, which can be discouraged by dressing with agricultural naphthaline at the rate of two ounces per square yard at seven days' intervals until the end of May.

Carrots for storing should never be pulled, but carefully lifted before frost can affect them, the leaves cut off about half an inch above the crown, and stored in clamps or boxes well covered with weathered ashes.

The Cauliflower resembles Broccoli but is less hardy, probably a little more mellow in flavour and has a wide range in the time of its maturity. It thrives best in a rich soil not too heavy in character. Early Cauliflowers can be produced by sowing in August and leaving the plants in frames until they can be planted out in February or until May, according to location and weather. Outdoor sowings should be made in April and May in prepared seed beds in a trench about four inches deep, which will render watering easy, and planted out in ranks two feet apart, with eighteen inches between the plants.

The seed is small and about 2,000 seeds make up an ounce. The well-known varieties are Early Snowball, All the Year Round, Walcheren, Veitch's Autumn Giant. Care should be taken not to plant out the "blind" plants which have no central green leaves. In some seasons the percentage of blind plants is very high, often reaching forty per cent. In really hot or stormy weather, the leaves may be bent over to protect the curds as they form.

Celeriac is the so-called turnip-rooted Celery, and is grown in deeply dug, well manured, rich soil, and can be stored in frost-proof boxes of dry sand. Seeds bulk about 2,500 to the ounce. It should be grown in March under glass and planted out in June in ranks one foot apart and with one foot between the plants. The leaves and stems may be used for flavouring and will impart the usual celery flavour to soups. Celeriac is a rich feeder and can be watered to advantage in dry weather.

The root should be lifted before frost intervenes, and stored as indicated.

The roots cooked like turnips and sliced make a very palatable salading; they can also be grated into dressing for salads, or salted and pickled in the same way as Red Cabbage.

Celery provides a test for the good gardener, and is a good and tasty vegetable. As it takes from six to nine months to mature, it should be sown under glass in March and planted out nine inches apart, in staggered ranks, in prepared trenches about eighteen inches wide and twelve inches deep, with the soil heaped up at the sides, and the soil in the trench enriched with well-rotted manure in June. Celery is very unpalatable unless well bleached, and earthing up should be started not later than early September, and continued until only the tops are visible. The new self-bleaching variety, however, takes the toil from the gardener's task, for it may be planted upon the surface in rich soil in serried ranks, not more than nine inches apart, and needs no earthing up. Its flavour is magnificent.

Celery will benefit by being dressed with soot, as this keeps slugs away. Storing is done by leaving the Celery in the ground, where in most seasons it can be kept until April. Seed bulks about five hundred to the ounce.

Chicory is a salad vegetable too seldom grown, which needs similar soil and conditions to Celery. The seed, which numbers about 1,500 to the ounce, is sown in the open in May, in rows fifteen inches apart, and thinned to nine inches apart in a shaded part of the garden. The leaves are blanched and eaten like lettuce, or picked while fresh and green and cooked in a similar manner to spinach. The roots may be cut into slices and served with salad.

Colewort, or the Collard Cabbage, is an excellent Brassica, which provides "Winter greens," and should be sown in July in the seed bed and transplanted to nine inches apart. The varieties Rosette or Cabbaging Colewort provide round heads similar to small cabbages and are resistant to very severe frost. They should be treated in exactly the same way as cabbages.

The Ridge Cucumber is a vegetable which has improved very considerably in recent years, and is now comparable in size and flavour with the Frame Cucumber. It can be grown in any well-manured soil in a moist site, preferably, as its name indicates, upon a mound of soil raised into the form of a ridge. Seeds are best sown singly in pots in the shelter of a cold frame in April. It should be planted out in mid May, and the leading shoot pinched out to encourage the production of side-shoots. On the whole a partially shaded site is best, and no attempt should be made to keep the bed clear of weeds, provided that the soil is sufficiently moist or watered. Watering should be copious when practised.

Endive is similar to Chicory in all its cultural needs.

Among the most prolific of all green vegetables are the Kales or Borecoles, which are almost free of trouble from the gardener's point of view.

All Kales prefer a heavy soil or really hard ground, and even if a crowbar is necessary to drive holes in the ground for planting, such ground should be preferred to a well-dug surface, in fact the line need only be drawn at the employment of dynamite for the purpose of making the necessary holes. Of course the plant should not be left floating upon an air cushion in the pocket so formed, and if necessary it should be filled with light, dry, friable soil.

Popular varieties are: Dwarf Green Curled, Tall Green Curled, Victoria Curled, Asparagus, Sutton's Favourite.

Early varieties are sown in the seed bed in March or April and planted out in June. The later varieties may be sown in June and planted out in September.

Kale should be cut while the leaves are young, and one should remember that the more often it is cut the greater the speed at which it will grow. An ounce of seed will provide about two thousand plants.

Kohl Rabi is sometimes known as the turnip-rooted cabbage, and provides a vegetable with whiter flesh and a sweeter flavour than the normal turnip. Impervious to frost; the seeds which number between 3-4,000 to the ounce, should be sown in good soil in rows fifteen inches apart, and thinned to nine inches apart, though the plants are transplantable. If transplanted, they should be puddled in the same way as all the Brassicas. The leaves, which may be cooked in the same way as spinach, have an exceptionally attractive flavour, but should be picked while still young.

Sowings should be made in April, and the swollen stems of the plant should be gathered when about the size of a tennis ball, for later they tend to become woody and hard.

Leeks, which are members of the Allium or Garlic family, are gross feeders and will consume with fervour all the various nutrients the gardener will offer them. Seeds may be sown as early as January in gentle heat and brought on until they are ready to plant out of doors in April, when they should be dibbered into a prepared and well-dug trench six inches deep and copiously manured. Fill the hole into which they are placed with water after planting, but don't worry to fill the hole in, the leeks will do that. The plants should be eight inches apart in staggered double rows, with eighteen inches between the double rows. Seeds number about five hundred to the ounce.

Onion Fly is the worst pest to affect the Leek, but it can be discouraged by dusting with a proprietary brand of Calomel. Its onset is most noticeable while the plants are small and can be distinguished by the yellowing of the leaves, and the subsequent whitening. Onion Smut is a notifiable disease which evinces its presence by a black, smutty stripe upon the lower part of the leaves.

Lettuce is a badly grown crop as a rule, coming as a glut only at one season of the year, instead of in steady succession.

The two varieties, Cabbage and Cos, are quite distinctive both in shape and flavour. On the whole they are best sown and thinned out as required upon rich, well-cultivated soil. With care however, both varieties can be transplanted. Shortening the tap root will often prevent them from "running up." Sowings should take place at regular fortnightly intervals to ensure a succession of crops. Spacing should be nine inches to one foot apart.

Of the Cabbage varieties, the early sowings should be confined to Sutton's Favourite, All the Year Round, May Queen, Tom Thumb, and Loos Tennis Ball. The autumn sowings should be made from Imperial, Arctic, Stanstead Park, and Trocadero.

Of the Cos varieties, Sutton's Winter White, Black-seeded

Bath, Paris White and Winter are a good selection. The Cos varieties need tying up to blanch and should be watched to see that they do not run to seed.

The best lettuce for growing in heated greenhouses or frames is undoubtedly Cheshunt Early Giant, produced by Dr. Bewlay at the Cheshunt Experimental and Research Station.

The story of its production is worth retelling. Market gardeners who concentrated upon the production of tomatoes in summer required a crop which would mature quickly in the winter months. The lettuce appeared to be the ideal crop, but no lettuce existed which would heart uniformly under the normal conditions of winter daylight. Certain Norwegian scientists had divided the known cultivated lettuces into three classes—those which would heart with 14-16 hours of daylight, those which would heart with 12-14 hours of daylight, and those which required 10-12 hours of daylight. Dr. Bewlay collected from all sources seeds of the latter class, and among a crop of some 16,000 lettuces found three lettuces which fulfilled the requirements of producing substantial hearts with the 8-10 hours of daylight normal to the winter months. These lettuces produced the parent seeds of the variety known as Cheshunt Early Giant. But that was not the end. Lettuces grown in this country dissipate their seeds under normal weather conditions, and it was necessary to grow the lettuces for seed in a country where the seed could be harvested in reasonable quantity. Dr. Bewlay visited Italy and tried Italian growers with but fair success, but eventually succeeded in obtaining a good yearly crop from well-known growers in California. Thus your winter lettuce is almost invariably grown from American seed.

A number of pests affect the Lettuce, many of which can be avoided by growing in well-drained soil. Slugs should be discouraged by the use of soot, or by such preparations as Slug-Death or Meta fuel crushed and mixed with damp tea leaves.

Marrows can be, like Field Marshals, either attractive or gross. The gross kinds win most medals! My own favourite is a kind called Rotherside Orange, which is seldom large, but round and golden both in skin and flesh, and of exquisite flavour. It produces its fruits quickly upon long strands of growth like golden strings of pearls. The bush type of vegetable marrow keeps closer in growth and is better suited to small gardens. They require a well-dug, well-drained, manured soil, and should be encouraged with liquid manure at regular intervals. The seeds number about 700 to the ounce.

The best trailing varieties are Rotherside Orange, Moore's Cream, Long Green, and Table Dainty; suitable bush varieties are Bush Green and Bush White.

Attractive variants of the Marrows are the Squashes, of which Hubbard's American Green and Hubbard's American Golden Squash are the best known. Cultivation is identical to that for Marrows, and the attractively coloured lemon-shaped fruits have firmer, sweeter and more deeply coloured flesh than that of the ordinary marrow.

The Custard Marrow, so called because of the shape of its fruits which resemble a baked custard with scalloped margins, is distinguished also by the more creamy texture of its cooked flesh, and is completely delicious when baked.

Seed should be sown in frames in April and the young hardened plants transplanted where they are to grow—about four feet apart—in June.

Mustard and Cress is perhaps the easiest of the salad crops to grow, and should be grown in rich soil in a shady place, since this will produce the long succulent white stems which make it palatable. The soil should be sifted and the surface should be light, and the seed sown thickly and separately, with the Cress three days before the Mustard. Both will then be ready at the same time if kept sufficiently moist. It should always be cut before it passes the cotyledon stage, that is to say, before it produces more than two leaves.

The secret of growing good onions lies in the early preparation of the beds. Well-rotted manure should be forked in about six inches below the surface, and soot should be worked into the upper surface. See that a very fine tilth is obtained by adequate forking and raking. Into the surface four inches of soil work a mixture of equal parts of dried blood and steamed bone flour at the rate of four ounces per square yard, adding wood-ash if available. Tread or roll down the surface to make it as firm as possible.

The first sowing should be made under glass early in February and the seedlings planted out in rows in the prepared bed in April, in rows twelve inches apart, with six inches between the plants. These should not be overlarge when planted out, and a good general rule should be to plant out onions when they are from two and a half to three inches in height.

Alternatively the seed may be sown in March in rows nine inches apart and thinned to six inches apart, the thinnings being used as salading. Plants may be fed with liquid manure until the end of July, when such feeding should cease. Maturity takes place at any time from August onwards, when the tops should be bent over at the summit of the bulb, each being bent in an alternative direction. Dusting with soot is still efficacious at this time. When the sun has ripened the bulbs they should be lifted and put into the sun to dry thoroughly. When the tops have become as dry as hay they may be plaited into a string and the string hung in a cool, dry, but frost-proof place. Pests affecting the Onion have been dealt with under Leek.

The best varieties for saladings are White Lisbon, or White Spanish.

For use during summer: Rousham Park, Hero, Giant Rocca, James's Keeping, White Spanish, and Cranston's Excelsior.

The best keeping varieties are Ailsa Craig, Bedfordshire Champion, Brown Globe, and Up-to-Date. The best pickling varieties are New Queen and Silver Skinned.

One ounce of seed should produce a one hundred and fifty foot run.

No problem arises from the storage of Parsnips, since they can be adequately stored in the ground; frost merely serving to improve them. Early sowing, preferably in mid-February, is recommended in ground which can be worked early in the year. Ground should be well and deeply dug but not freshly manured, and the seed should be patch-sown in groups of from three to four seeds at intervals of nine inches in a drill one and a half inches deep, in rows fifteen inches apart. All but the strongest seedling in each patch should be eradicated. The best varieties for garden purposes are Tender and True, Hollow Crown, and Offenham.

Peas are one of the most interesting crops from the gardener's point of view, both gastronomically and horticulturally. They store well and are high in food value.

The ideal soil is one well enriched with humus, well limed and deeply dug. A good plan is to dig into the prepared bed all the grass cuttings available, and to dress the site well with super-phosphate of lime before sowing at the rate of three ounces per square yard. For preference seeds should be sown in belts twelve inches wide, with the individual seeds three inches apart, so that sixteen seeds occupy a square foot of soil. Peas should be rolled in red lead mixed in water before sowing, to discourage the attentions of marauding mice!

In protected districts the first sowing may be done in March but the main sowings should not be made until April. The early varieties mature about twelve weeks after sowing, the second earlies in thirteen to fourteen weeks, and the later varieties in about fifteen weeks.

The best dwarf early varieties are: Kelvedon Wonder, Peter Pan, Pioneer, Meteor, Little Marvel, Marvellous; the taller and second early varieties: Gradus, Laxton's Progress, Admiral Beatty, Foremost, Pilot, Duke of York, and Sutton's Supreme.

The main crop varieties are Onward, Duke of Albany, Peerless, Dreadnought, and Giant Stride.

The late Peas are: Autocrat, Ne Plus Ultra, Late Duke, and Alderman.

The pests affecting peas are those indicated under Broad Beans.

Pea sticks should be used at the earliest moment when growth indicates that they are necessary. Peas for storage should be picked while young and blanched and dried as indicated for Broad Beans.

A good base for soups may be made by boiling the young pods.

The sugar pea is an interesting variative, grown in identical fashion, but the whole pod is cooked while still young and peas yet unformed. The flavour of the cooked pods is that of asparagus, nutritive value is exceptional.

The Potato is the indispensable vegetable, and the primary crop for all newly dug gardens. The ideal soil is one that is rich, and the site should be one which is open to light, sun, and air. Light soils should be enriched with well-decayed humus.

16.  "There is beauty in even the Red Cabbage"

Heavy soils should be well dug, with straw well dug in, in the autumn and left to benefit from winter frosts.

Superphosphate of lime at the rate of two ounces per square yard is an adequate fertiliser, and as potatoes thrive in a slightly acid soil, no extensive application of lime should be made to the soil.

The number of varieties is legion, and any selection would necessarily be trivial. Indication is therefore made only of typical varieties.

Of these the early varieties are Arran Pilot, Duke of York, Epicure, and Sharpe's Express.

Second early varieties: Arran Banner, Arran Comrade, Doon Star, and Majestic.

Main crop: Great Scot, Arran Consul, Catriona, and Golden Wonder.

Before planting the seed should be sprouted, as this makes a considerable difference to the crop. The seed of most varieties should average eight to the pound, though in the case of such early varieties as Sharpe's Express the average is nearer six. All damaged or unhealthy seed should be rejected. The seed should be placed in shallow trays in a light, dry, frost-proof room with the end of the potato showing the most eyes to the top. The aim should be to get two or three strong shoots nicely greened before planting, and any in excess of this number should be rubbed off.

It is interesting to note how much the modern cultivation of the potato varies from garden practice of more than a hundred years ago.

A reputable gardener's dictionary of the year 1802 gives the following method. The seed potato should be the largest of the previous year's crop. It should be cut into at least 12 pieces, each bearing one eye. As the haulm grows it is continually covered with successive layers of soil, so that it continues to produce more and more runners. Under such circumstances the parent potato is often credited with progeny weighing up to four cwts. One day I intend to try the method, but so far I haven't managed it.

The quantity of seed potatoes required for a given patch of ground can easily be calculated from the data given.

Early potatoes should be planted in late March, second earlies in the first week in April, and the main crop not later than the third week of that month.

On the whole the best method of planting is to turn back the soil in the form of a trench which should be slightly deeper in light soils than in heavy ones, to give a depth (in heavy soils) of four inches, with a space of thirty inches between the trenches.

The second and early varieties should be planted twelve to fifteen inches apart, the soil being drawn up in the form of a ridge. Earthing up should begin before the tops have grown sufficiently to touch. The crop takes approximately fourteen weeks to mature, so that the earlies should be ready during June, the second earlies in July, and the main crop in August. The main crop varieties should not be lifted until the haulm has died down.

The list of diseases and pests which affect the potato is depressing—so are those affecting the human race. It is comforting to think that many people die of old age! Pests which inhabit the soil can be discouraged with whizzed naphthaline. Wart disease (to which many varieties are immune) shows itself as a cauliflower-like growth on stem and root. It is a serious disease and generally speaking it is better to keep to the immune varieties. The disease is notifiable, as is of course the advent of the Colorado Beetle.

The Scab Disease of potatoes does not render them unfit for consumption, but makes the crop wasteful to consume, and is most prevalent in light soils and those freshly reclaimed from grass. Liming the soil frequently encourages the disease.

The final disease is Potato Blight, *Phythophora infestans*, which usually makes its presence felt in wet weather. A disease of fungoid origin, the speed of its encroachment is very great. Blackening of the leaves and collapse of the haulm signifies its presence, and if the disease spreads to the tubers, they fail to keep. Spraying, except in industrial districts, with Bordeaux mixture will prevent the onset of the disease, and certain colloidal copper sprays are equally effective. Potato Blight must be effectively controlled in all gardens in which tomatoes are also grown, as it spreads also to them. Here spraying the tomatoes at intervals of nine days with a colloidal copper spray is recommended.

Potatoes should be carefully dug when the weather is fine and the soil dry. A day in the sun generally renders them fit to store, which, if the quantity is small can be done in bags, provided they are kept in a dry, frost-proof place. For larger quantities a clamp is most suitable.

The Radish is a good salad vegetable, which, to be palatable, should mature in not more than three weeks. It should be used as a catch crop between other varieties—the Beet, Parsnip, and Carrot, for instance.

As a change, try the Black Spanish and China Rose Radishes, which should be sown in late August or early September. These grow to a larger size than the ordinary radish. The tops, which can be used as greens, are very palatable, and the roots can be stored throughout the winter. Cut in thin slices, these may be consumed uncooked, or alternatively may be cooked in the same way as the turnip.

The Shallot is particularly free from pests and diseases, being unaffected by the Onion Fly. It should be planted in well-dug soil to which two ounces of superphosphate per square yard has been added, with the addition of a good dressing of wood-ash or, if available, one ounce of potassium sulphate per square yard.

The "cloves" as they are sometimes called, should be planted in late February and be pushed firmly into the soil so that they are half covered. Planted in rows one foot apart, with nine inches between the bulbs, a six-fold increase can generally be anticipated. They are normally ready to be lifted in September, when they should be well dried in the sun before being placed in bags for winter storage.

Three kinds of Spinach—now much popularised in song and cartoon—can be grown in the average garden. Perpetual Spinach or Spinach Beet as it is generally called, can be a very good and lucrative crop under trees in the orchard, and can be cut as often as one desires. The summer and winter varieties should be used in the same way as radishes, as a catch crop, only a small quantity being sown at a time. The summer varieties are sown in drills nine inches apart, and thinned out to six inches between the plants. Periods for sowing are between

March and late June. The winter variety should be sown in the same way from July to September. Perpetual Spinach should be sown at any time from April to August in drills fifteen inches apart, and thinned to the same distance. Remember, when cooking any type of Spinach, that the leaves should not be cut with a knife but torn apart; that they require no water other than that which adheres to them from the washing which they will have needed.

The ribs or stalks of Perpetual Spinach are extremely tasty and should be cooked separately in a similar way to Asparagus.

Swedes are a comparatively trouble-free crop. Sown in soil manured only for a previously grown crop, they should be sown at the end of May in shallow drills one foot apart, and thinned to nine inches apart.

Sweet Corn is one of the least grown but most satisfying of the less usual vegetables, but if your palate is delicate it is most unwise to spare your pocket the expense entailed by expending a few coppers upon the seed of a reputable table variety by culling a few maize seeds from chicken food and experimenting with it, since, though you may produce large cobs, the smaller cobs obtained from the recognised table varieties are much sweeter and certainly of fuller flavour.

Recent investigation leads one to suppose that symbiosis exists between the microrhiza of the sweet corn and those of the tomato, and one may yet look forward to the sweet corn being grown to provide the stake to which to tie the tomato, and both growing better in this conjunction than they would in isolation.

Reverting, however, to the Sweet Corn for your garden. Choose a variety like Golden Sunrise or D.S.H. and if you wish to raise an early crop soak the seeds in water for twenty-four hours, plant three seeds in each small pot, place in a frame in mid-April, and plant out the contents of each pot separately at intervals of two feet between each group of three plants. Experience has shown that thus planted, larger and more certain crops are obtained than if planted single. If the earliness of the crop is of no moment, plant the seeds out in groups of three, two feet between each group, in rows three feet apart, at the end of April.

Tomatoes are frequently a very satisfactory outdoor crop.

To succeed if plants are to be raised from seed, these should be thinly sown in a seed pan during the first week in March in a greenhouse whose temperature is not allowed to fall below 45°F. The typical soil for the purpose should consist of sterilised loam two parts, coarse sand one part, sterilised peat one part, to which should be added superphosphate of lime at the rate of one quarter ounce per gallon, with the addition of one-eighth of an ounce of powdered chalk per gallon.

When the plants show their second leaves they should be potted in two and a half-inch pots and grown steadily on, and once again potted on into four and a half inch pots as soon as the roots completely occupy the smaller pots. The aim should be to get the first truss of flowers showing colour before they are planted out. Toward the end of April they should be gradually hardened off, and planted out during May. Plants, if healthy, should be dark green in colour, and short and stocky, and on one stem. Side shoots should be rubbed out as soon as they develop, and the plant firmly staked and tied.

The best fertiliser to use in the soil before planting is plenty of wood-ash, or sulphate of potash at the rate of two ounces per square yard, with steamed bone flour at double this rate. When the first truss of fruit has set, a balanced fertiliser (there are many of these upon the market) should be applied at the indicated rate, and with regularity. Side shoots should be rubbed out and the plants tied to stout stakes about five feet in height.

The ripening of tomatoes is brought about by chemical action, and not essentially by sunlight, so that the only leaves which should be removed are those which prevent a free circulation of air, or those which are withering. The gardener's problem is to keep the plants growing actively, and to this end he should take steps to see that they do not become suddenly "dried out" in spells of hot weather, and he should *not* "stop" them by pinching out the main stem after four trusses have been formed, as a plant in active growth is more likely to complete its life's work than one which has been rendered more or less moribund.

The most serious diseases which affect the tomato may be divided into three classes:

    a.  the fungoid diseases—due to bacterial infection, usually windborne.

b.  the virus diseases—diseases of the sap—carried generally by touch, or inherited from the seed.

c.  the mosaic diseases—generally due to lack of effective balance in the soil, or incorrect feeding.

It will be sufficient for our purpose to indicate the procedure to be followed in the case of each type of disease.

a.  The most typical of the fungoid diseases is the Potato Blight, or Phytophora infestans, which indicates its own onset by a blackening of the leaves, and by a bronzy-black encirclement of the stems. It spreads rapidly, attacks even the fruits, and renders them unfit to eat or to store. Fortunately the disease almost always shows itself in the potato haulms first, and its onset can be prevented by spraying at regular intervals of nine days with a wash of Bouissol, or of Bordeaux or Burgundy mixture, but it must be done with regularity, and all the new growth and the fruits must be adequately covered at each spraying.

In the green-house Cladosporium fulvum (the Tomato leaf mould) is an almost certain visitor, and of like origin. A similar wash is used for spraying. The variety Vetomold is immune and is a very good cropper.

b.  Of the virus diseases, a typical example is Stringy Virus, which shows itself by the attenuation of the leaves, so that they become string-like. The disease may be inborn or contracted, and carried from plant to plant by the gardener's fingers or his knife, or by contact. Infected plants should be up-rooted and destroyed, care being taken not to touch the other plants, and the hands should be well washed, and the knife, if used, dipped in the copper wash.

c.  Mosaic diseases are caused by an upset in the internal economy of the plant, by inadequate or unsuitable feeding, and show themselves by mottling of the leaves, and marbling of the fruits. Uneven ripening and green-back in the fruits on ripening are usually attributed to this cause, and can be cured by the adequate use of potash.

One of the most usual causes of failure in the amateur's garden is the cracking and splitting of fruits, and this can be obviated by adequate watering while the plants are growing, since it is always the result of a check imparted by a period of drought, and followed by periods of ample moisture.

No problem presents itself in the picking of the ripe fruits, but the ripening of the green fruits still left upon the plants in October is important. These should be picked, if the quantity is large, in trusses, dipped in the Bouissol spray, and allowed to drain and dry. They should then be placed upon straw and covered with another layer of straw and kept in a darkened store-room in which the temperature is maintained at between fifty and sixty degrees Fahrenheit.

If the quantity is smaller, the green fruits, after drying, should be placed in a box containing dry peat moss litter, or dry sawdust, and kept in a warm dry place, being looked over at regular intervals to extract those which have ripened.

Plants which have been badly affected with Potato Blight produce fruits which will not store or keep, even though they appear sound, and such fruits should be converted into chutney or cooked and consumed while still green.

The best varieties for outdoor culture are: Potentate, Essex Wonder, Carter's Sunrise, Open Air, Ailsa Craig, and Maincrop.

For indoor growing: Market Queen, Potentate, Vetomold (not subject to Leaf Mould).

A very good dwarf variety is Harrison's First in the Field.

It seems a great pity that a much publicised "new" bush tomato should be hailed as a "labour saving" tomato. It certainly has many good points but one could hardly justify growing it upon the grounds of the alleged labour saved, since, like every other tomato, it must be adequately "stopped" or it will become a wizened wildling. For outdoor cropping it is not a good variety, as it is exceptionally thin skinned, and the fruits are liable to crack; but it does give a remarkable crop of really good fruits under indoor conditions, and is an excellent addition to the ranks of the tomatoes.

Seed is approximately 1,600 to each ounce, and germination usually exceeds 90 per cent.

The Turnip, is a member of the Brassica family and for rotation purposes, should be regarded as belonging to the great tribe. Turnips fare best in light soil which is not too rich but has been well limed and dressed with superphosphate at the rate of two ounces to the square yard. Wood-ash dressing is very beneficial and a dressing of one ounce of sulphate of potash and two ounces of sulphate of ammonia is also to be desired.

Sowing should be made in April or May for autumn-maturing crops, and in June for winter crops. Approximately one ounce of seed is required to sow a 150 feet run, and should be put in shallow drills, one foot apart, with the plants thinned to six inches apart. Dry weather has the effect of making the plants run to seed, and in the garden at least the growing turnips should be watered during long dry spells.

Pests are the same as those for the Brassicas, and can be discouraged by dusting with soot. Additional inconvenience can be accorded the Turnip Fly by spreading grass cuttings around the rows of young seedlings.

It should not be forgotten that the tops of winter turnips are exceptionally good greens. Storage is identical with that for carrots.

To conclude upon a general note: grow what you will, where you can; learn from your mistakes and your successes; never neglect to experiment, for it is in this way real gardeners are made.

One is not too young at two years of age to be a gardener, and the centenarian gardener probably realises better than any other that there is still much more to learn than he has already absorbed.

THE END

# INDEX

153